For my daughter Christie,
a wonderful new mommy—
four times within four years, no less

Contents

Acknowledgments

This book was inspired by my daughter Christine, who finally realized her lifelong dream of being a mother with the births of John in 2004, Ryan in 2006, and twins Fynn and Dylan in 2008. Thank you, sweetheart, for giving me such beautiful, delightful grandboybies and for allowing me to tag along on your incredible journey of motherhood.

As always, I am grateful for the terrific team at Adams Media for contributing their talents and professionalism and enthusiasm to this book. A special tip of the hat goes to Meredith O'Hayre, *Cup of Comfort®* project editor; Carol Goff, the book's copy-editor; Ashley Vierra, the book's designer; Jacquinn Williams, publicist; and Paula Munier, creator and champion of the *Cup of Comfort®* book series.

I am amazed by and profoundly thankful to the authors whose stories grace these pages. Each has been an inspiration and a joy to work with.

And thank you, dear readers, for allowing us to share these very special stories about the most miraculous experience on Earth: having a baby.

Introduction

"As often as I have witnessed the miracle, held the perfect creature with its tiny hands and feet, each time I have felt as though I were entering a cathedral with prayer in my heart."

Margaret Sanger

No other experiences in my life have confirmed the existence of God and felt more sacred to me than giving birth to each of my three children and witnessing the birth of my first grandchild. And though I wasn't able to witness the actual births of my granddaughter or my other four grandsons, I held each of them within the first twenty-four hours of their births and felt that same deep connection to them and to God. Each time I even hear of another soul entering our world through the womb of a woman, the miracle and the beauty of childbirth take my breath away.

Then reality—and with it, worry—sets in. Because, for starters, I'm a natural-born, first-class worrywart. And because I know from firsthand experience and from the experiences of family and friends and complete strangers that motherhood brings not only an endless stream of blessings but also a whole litany of challenges. Pregnancy, childbirth, and being the mother of a brand-new baby, or babies (as my daughter Christie is experiencing right now), is a great big bagful of experiences and mixed emotions unlike any that a woman will encounter in her entire life.

For me, one of the most difficult parts of being a new mom, way back then, was hearing all the horror stories from well-meaning experienced mothers as well as from people, women and men alike, who'd never had a child but, for some reason, felt compelled to share their "knowledge" with me. Another difficulty was trying to sift through a great deal of conflicting information (much of it misinformation, it turned out) that, again, I received—some of it bidden, much of it unbidden—from well-meaning folks, everyone from close familiars to total strangers. Only long after the fact, after the pregnancies, births, and infancies of my three children and the loss of a baby to miscarriage, did it occur to me that each of my experiences had been unique—unique to each child, unique to me, different from the experiences of every other mother and child on Earth.

Yet, there are also similarities in all new-mom experiences. And there is something—indeed, much— to be gained from sharing our personal new-mom experiences with one another. There is strength, knowledge, inspiration, and comfort to be had in hearing, or reading, about another woman who has walked in your shoes, who has had a similar experience and felt similar emotions—especially when those stories are spot-on and told in a positive way. There is, as Elizabeth King Gerlach's story so eloquently states, "a sisterhood of motherhood."

The uplifting stories in this collection personify the sisterhood of new mothers and celebrate the unparalleled miracle of bringing a new baby into your life. I hope these stories bring you much comfort and joy.

Colleen Sell

Delivering Hope

I grabbed hold of my abdomen as it tightened. This was more intense than the "false labor" I'd had days earlier. Excited, I knew I'd soon be holding our first baby in my arms. I grabbed the phone and punched in my mother-in-law's number, hoping to give her plenty of time to get in to the city. Since this was her first grandchild, we wanted to share the experience with her.

"Katie, turn on the television," my mother-in-law said, her voice somber.

I picked up the remote and clicked it on, then watched in horror as the scene in my front yard unfolded.

I banged down the phone and hurried to the roof of our twenty-eight-story apartment building. My mother, who had already come to help with the baby, followed. A mass of onlookers crowded together, staring in disbelief at the inferno one mile south. Several people took pictures, certain that if they did not lock in this moment, it would seem too far-fetched to believe at a later date.

"I've got to go wake Larry," I told Mom.

I rushed to the elevator and took it down to our second-floor apartment. When Larry and I returned to the roof, we found Mom sitting on a ledge in tears. She'd just witnessed the second plane crash into tower two of the World Trade Center.

"Planes were hijacked," someone said.

We stared, confused, wondering what would be hit next. Amidst the unfolding tragedy, my joy of giving birth had transformed into a deep fear. In mere minutes, the world had clouded over and become a dark, terrifying place.

I stood beside Larry and watched the towers as they collapsed into a dense cloud of gray that moved toward us as if in slow motion, like the effect of some massive movie explosion. I prayed that two of our dear friends had made it out alive.

Later that afternoon, my husband, mother, and I walked ten blocks south to my doctor's office for a scheduled appointment. The walk took on a nightmarish quality as we watched people trudge north up Park Avenue. Hundreds of men and women in dust-covered suits and shoes, their faces dusted white, plodded toward their homes. At least forty ambulances and fire trucks passed, sirens blaring, all from Long Island, three hours away. The realization hit me that these firefighters and paramedics had volunteered to enter one of the United States' worst disasters ever. I sat down on the curb and wept, then pulled myself together enough to finish our walk.

Later that evening, after we returned home from the doctor visit, we learned that both our friends had survived the tragedy, along with several of their coworkers, all of whom had been away from the WTC at a meeting in midtown. Still, we knew of at least twelve acquaintances unaccounted for.

Two days later, on September 13, my contractions intensified enough that I knew it was time to go to the hospital. No taxis were operating through that section of Manhattan, so again the three of us began the ten-block trek. The contractions grew closer and stronger, forcing me to periodically stop and rest. People looked at us forlornly and sympathetically, perhaps assuming we were searching for someone. They couldn't know the emotional angst that surged within me.

Our beautiful city looked like a war zone. Debris littered the streets and sidewalks. Parked cars covered in gray looked like stone statues. People everywhere wore looks of despair as they sought missing loved ones. I cried inside for those people and for the victims, but at the same time, I felt a secret rejoicing. I was on my way to give birth, to meet this baby I had anticipated for months. Then, without warning, my heart would nose-dive as I wondered what the future held for my child, for all of us.

We walked past bars overflowing with people. They weren't celebrating, though; they were just huddled together, quietly sharing the sorrow and contemplating the reason for this attack on innocent lives. At First Avenue, we paused near barricades that blocked the street. When we saw that many people were wandering around carrying locks of hair and dental records, we knew they were waiting to get into the morgue.

Closer to the hospital, another intense contraction forced me to stop.

"Are you okay?" an officer approached. "Are you looking for someone?"

Again, my distress was mistaken. I looked at him, trying to mask the pain.

"No, I'm in labor." I breathed heavily, the birth pains coming faster.

The officer quickly produced a wheelchair. My husband hurried, pushing me toward the hospital, but at the entrance, the line for blood donors stretched out the door. Carefully, we weaved our way through the crowd only to find every birthing room full. Another contraction came, and I knew it was time. Instead of the comfort of a birthing room and the familiarity of my doctor, I was prepped and gave birth in the operating room at the hands of a doctor I hadn't met.

I'd imagined it so differently. Where was the happy celebration, the looking forward to the future for my husband, our baby, and me? Larry sat next to the bed while I held Jack in my arms. Other couples in the hospital did the same, swimming in an ebb and flow of mixed emotions: joy over the lives we'd brought into the world, yet unable to tear our eyes and our minds from the tragedy outside the hospital windows.

"It's bittersweet, isn't it," I said to Larry as I stared into my newborn son's perfect little face, "that amidst all this tragedy, the most beautiful miracle has happened for us."

Although he remained silent, I knew Larry agreed by the gentleness in his touch as he placed a finger in Jack's tiny fist. Today, I think of Jack's birth as a symbol of hope—a bright spot to look toward during dark times. Just as new growth rejuvenates the earth after a forest fire, so too do I now see my son's unfolding life as a beautiful part of a better tomorrow.

Tammera Ayers, as told by Cathy Chasin

This story was first published in the e-zine Melody of the Heart, *April 2003.*

A Tale of Two Mothers

The battle began while I was still in the hospital. As I lay in bed, trying to follow the nurse's instructions to shove what seemed like my entire breast into the sweet, rosebud mouth of my two-day-old son, the phone rang. I knew it would be my mother, calling to check on her youngest daughter and seventh grandchild for the millionth time that day. I couldn't fault her itchy dialing finger; Teodor was my first child, and we were more than 3,000 miles away in France. If she could have crawled through the telephone wires to get to us, she would have.

"Hey, Mom."

"Hi, sweetie! What are you up to?"

"Trying to feed Teo," I answered, wincing slightly as my little one latched on and began to suck vigorously. *Too vigorously? Why was he sucking so hard?*

I wondered, frowning down at him. *Was he latched on correctly? Was he getting anything? Was I producing anything? Might I be starving my baby?*

My mother interrupted my silent, spiraling freak-out with a gasp. "What?"

"Huh?" I said.

"You're feeding him again?" She sounded incredulous.

My thoughts changed course so fast, I could almost feel my brain slam into my skull. *Was I over-feeding my baby? Was he eating too much? Would I make him sick?*

I began to babble excuses. "It's been two hours . . . He was crying . . . I don't think my milk has come in yet . . . The nurses say it's good to feed him often at first to get him into the habit of eating." I stopped, confused.

"Well, I don't think you're supposed to feed him that often," my mother said comfortably. "At least, that's not what we did when you were a baby. Every three to four hours, as I recall, is right."

There. Right there. After barely forty-eight hours of motherhood, I had reached the infamous milestone every new parent hopes to skip, the "that's not what we did when you were a baby" tug-of-war. The baby books had warned me. Friends had warned me. Even my prenatal infant care course instructor had warned me. So, intellectually, I knew that it was very common for grandparents to question the decisions of new parents, from whether to lay a sleeping baby on his back or his stomach, to how warmly to dress the child, to whether to breastfeed or bottle-feed. But actually hearing this phrase had an unexpected effect on me. As she spoke, I could feel my limbs shrinking, my hair twisting into pigtails, and the child in my arms becoming no more than a living doll.

As a thirty-something, married, professional woman, I was shocked that a few casual words from my mother could trigger such a rapid regression. I had thought that my maternal instincts would trump any girlish impulse I had to automatically cancel my own opinion in favor of hers. But I was wrong. I hadn't counted on the fact that my mother's doubtful voice would closely echo the one in my head that told me I wasn't a real mom.

In my opinion, there are a few ways to handle this sort of situation. One is to simply let your parent's words bead up and slide off you, like rain off a slicker. A second way is to gently but firmly say that, while whatever she did was obviously best when you were a child, times have changed. Third, you can become defensive, explosive, and stonily sure of yourself. Me, I went for option three. I was determined to prove to her—and yes, to myself—that I was no longer a little girl who needed her mother's advice or approval. I was a mother myself now and a very competent one, thank you very much!

My mother, however, remained oblivious to my stampy-foot demand to be treated like an adult. In fact, perhaps having something of her own to prove, she became more opinionated and dogged than ever. Although she wouldn't be coming to Paris for another two weeks—ostensibly to give my husband and me time to get used to being a family—we were on the phone so often, she might as well have been perched on the edge of my bed. I felt as if she had a comment (negative) for everything.

When the nurse brought me paracetamol for my episiotomy pain, she said, "Medicine? Are you sure it won't hurt the baby? That's not what we . . ."

"It's not cocaine, Mom," I snapped. "Just Tylenol."

We began bickering. We began arguing. We shed tears.

"Stop criticizing me!" I wailed, still in my hospital bed.

"I'm only trying to help!" she wept. "I don't know how much you know about all this!"

I began to dread her visit, which depressed me, because even though she was getting on my nerves,

I missed her. There was a part of me that very much needed my mom around for my first baby, I just couldn't remember why.

Before her visit, we made an uneasy truce. She agreed to try not to do what I perceived as criticism so much, and I agreed to try not to view it as criticism. We greeted each other joyfully, and she was full of kisses and hugs for her newest grandson. She used her jet lag to my advantage, holding and watching the baby while I slept. And she tried her best to keep her word. Sometimes I would see her literally biting her lip as I held the baby a certain way or did something that she wouldn't have done.

But one day, as I applied Lansinoh, given to me by the hospital, to my poor sore, cracked nipples, it was all too much for her.

"I don't think," she ventured tentatively, "that stuff is good for the baby."

Then it all started again. "You hold him too much." "You don't use his pacifier enough." "I really, really don't think you should be using that on your nipples."

Knowing that she didn't mean to criticize me didn't make me feel better. Feeling caught between a little girl and my thirty-something self, I split the difference and began to act like a rebellious teen: I slathered on Lansinoh liberally and ostentatiously.

I made whispered, closeted calls to the pediatrician. And, beyond all else, I would not share my confusion, my fears, my absolute vulnerability with her.

The turning point came one day when Teodor, who had been, until then, a fairly easy baby, started crying and wouldn't stop. I rocked him, I shushed him, I nursed him, I changed him, I patted him, and I pedaled his little legs—but nothing doing. He was unhappy and not one thing I did was making him better. For the first time, I began to feel overwhelmed. Every particle of my being was desperate to help him, but I didn't know how.

Finally, I gave up. I simply sat on my bed and held my wailing baby in my arms, trying my best to comfort him without breaking down into sobs myself. My mom, who had been unusually quiet during all this, came into my bedroom, and said, "Let me hold him . . . not that I think I can do it better than you."

As I handed my unhappy baby to my mother, I was ready to acknowledge defeat. I was sure the baby would stop crying in my mother's arms because she was Mom, and—who was I kidding?—I might have had a baby, but I wasn't yet a mother. Teodor, I figured, would know a real mom when he felt one.

But Teo didn't stop crying, even in my mother's arms. After a few seconds, my mother looked at me and gently placed the baby back in my arms. She left the room without another word, and a moment later, I heard her rattling around in the kitchen. I returned my attention to my baby, feeling vaguely reassured. He was not crying due to my ineptitude.

About a half-hour later, with the baby having finally drifted off into hiccupy sleep, I dragged myself out of the bedroom, exhausted and disheartened. But as I entered the hall, I encountered a familiar, spicy scent. My spirits rising, I followed the fragrance to the kitchen. And there, amid sparkling clean appliances, was my mother, taking a batch of warm, freshly made gingersnaps out of the oven—my favorite cookie, ever since childhood. I was so grateful for this quiet show of support that I nearly burst into tears. This was exactly the kind of mothering that I had needed and craved all along. The mom that was there for me, not only for my son. And for the first time since my mom had come to visit, I thought with shaky relief, *Oh, thank God, my mother is here.*

I'm not sure why, but that crying incident seemed to click something in place for both me and my mother. The rest of the visit was wonderful. As I learned to be Teo's mother, my own mother stood back and was just who I needed her to be—my mom, not a surrogate mom for Teodor. And I allowed myself to be the little girl who still very much needed her mommy to make things okay with a cookie. Finally, we had found our proper roles, and, as it turns out, they were the same roles that we'd had all along. Despite all our initial posturing, my becoming Teo's mother didn't change that fundamental relationship after all.

During the remainder of her visit, we played with the baby, giggled over romantic comedies, and read my infant care books together. She learned what I was basing my decisions on, and with her showing interest in why I was making the decisions I did, I was relaxed enough to ask her advice about child-rearing and share my insecurities about motherhood. And we ate cookies. My God, did we eat cookies. By the time she left, I had gained five pounds. Seven months later, I'm still struggling to lose them.

But that's a whole 'nother battle.

Barbara D. Diggs

Mother's First Year

As far back as I can remember I wanted to be a mother. Not just a mother, but the best mother ever. Where this compelling lust for motherhood came from, I have no idea. My own mother certainly didn't contribute to this deep-seated longing of mine in any way. She had trouble differentiating between children and dogs, believing that both should spend as much time outdoors as possible. So when my first daughter, Christina, was born, I made a solemn vow to become the Mother of All Mothers. I would be patient, kind, understanding, devoted, sacrificing, loving . . . everything and anything my child needed . . . at all times. I swore to uphold my duties as a mother with enthusiasm and joy.

Then we brought Christina home.

Suddenly, I had more questions than answers. I possessed all the ingredients for maternal panic:

first baby, no clue, stark terror. In spite of the sea of knowledge I had acquired by reading child-care books from cover to cover, I still had several questions, mostly what-ifs. I didn't feel confident enough to follow the good doctor's recommendation, to trust my instincts. What if I didn't have any?

On the first day home from the hospital, I carried my new bundle of joy into our bedroom and gently placed her upon the soft, pretty pink mattress in the newly painted white bassinet. I stepped back to marvel at the preciousness of my sleeping angel, and with my new-mother's smile still upon my face, I watched in horror as the bassinet suddenly collapsed on to the floor! And down came baby, bassinet and all. The sudden jolt caused Christina to wake up, which, in turn, caused her to start crying, which, in turn, caused me to feel like an immediate failure, which, in turn, caused me to start crying as well. This was not what I had envisioned as the perfect homecoming. Thus, day one began. And so did those mysterious headaches. The nervous twitch came later.

On day two, with less than two hours of sleep, a wailing infant, and a huge anxious knot in my stomach, I wanted to rethink things. The word "adoption" kept coming to mind. After another hour of restless writhing and crying from my wee one, abandonment came to mind. Then my head cleared. *What was I thinking? What kind of horrible mother am I?* Shocked by such evil thoughts, I experienced another first: Mother's Guilt. Now I had become, officially, a real mom. Unknown to me at the time, the invisible letter G would be branded on my forehead for all eternity. All future sources of pain, disappointment, and frustration experienced by my child could, and would, be traced back to me.

When Christina's sobbing had finally faded to mere whimpering, I figured I had passed the crisis. I smelled victory. I had survived the long night and won.

I was wrong.

After placing the tired, hiccupping, half-asleep infant in her bed, I quietly made my way to the door. Once safely outside the room, I slowly eased the door shut. Pressing my ear against the closed door, I held my breath and waited. I couldn't hear a thing. Not a sound. Relieved, I finally allowed myself to exhale. I had only one thought: get to the couch and fall on it.

It must have been the first step that did it. I never got the chance to put down my other foot. The explosive cry from inside the room pierced the walls, taking a shortcut through my heart. Frantic, I rushed back into the bedroom, expecting to find my precious baby being attacked by a horrible monster who had been secretly lurking in the closet. And it would be my fault. I hadn't checked the room for intruders. I ran over to her bassinet and looked down. To my great relief, I saw Christina still lying there unharmed. Nothing seemed out of the ordinary; she was simply maintaining her normal level of wailing.

Chiding myself for overreacting, I told myself to calm down. I tried to think in a cool, calm, and practical way. What could be the problem? She had been fed, burped, changed, walked, rocked, sang to. But the little red face looking up at me didn't seem impressed by any of those facts. Puzzled, I bent over and picked her up. The crying suddenly ceased. I lowered her again; the crying began. *Aha!* I thought. *So this is how it works.* I looked down on my little cherub; she looked solemnly up at me. We spent a minute or so sizing each other up. Something told me that this was a crucial moment in our lives. Instinct told me not to show fear. I stared boldly back into her tiny blue eyes, trying desperately not to blink. An important ancient ritual of sorts was taking place, and I knew it was imperative that I did not break the gaze. At last, I triumphed. Baby Christina broke the spell. Letting out a loud sigh, she yawned, closed her eyes, and fell fast asleep.

Feeling extremely proud of myself for holding my ground, I laid her gently back down into the bassinet and walked confidently out of the room. *She knows I'm the mom*, I thought smugly, closing the door behind me. I never saw the sly, satisfied smile that played at the corners of Christina's mouth as she slept.

My premature smugness evaporated during the coming weeks as I realized my life had somehow begun to resemble a form of basic training. My drill sergeant: Baby Christina. Reveille began at 2:00 A.M.; followed by another at 5:00 A.M. Eight o'clock was up for grabs. I marched to any tune Christina played, and if I fell out of step, she let me know right away. Days became a blur as I stumbled from bed to refrigerator, from stove to rocking chair, from diaper pail to laundry room. I lost all sense of time, living only for those rare moments between feedings and diaper changes, when feeding myself meant throwing down two pieces of bread and calling it a sandwich.

I hardly recognized my husband. He became that awful man who slept all night in my bed, undisturbed.

"So what if you have to get up for work at six o'clock in the morning?" I'd scream hysterically. "*You* have a life!"

Get a grip, Nancy, I'd tell myself over and over. *After all, this is what being a mother is all about. Someday, she'll thank me.*

I also believed pigs could fly.

One day, my own mother, sensing my need for some consolation and motherly advice, told me, "This, too, shall pass." When I asked her how long it would take to pass, she merely shrugged. Her wisdom only went so deep, so I didn't press. Besides, I figured that sooner or later Christina would have to sleep through the night, wouldn't she?

No. But I didn't know that then. Good thing. Hope is a terrible thing to lose.

My wardrobe changed after Christina's arrival as well. I found that I wore one basic accessory: a cloth diaper draped dramatically over my left shoulder. It went with everything. After a while, I actually became quite attached to this piece of cloth, feeling underdressed if it wasn't adorning my shoulder.

I began to smell funny, too. The persistent aroma of baby spit-up seemed to permeate my presence. It followed me everywhere. I smelled it as I cleaned, when I shopped, as I showered, even in my sleep. It became my "signature" scent. The aroma defined me.

At nine months, Christina learned the fine art of finger-painting. She painted her crib, the

the wall next to her crib, and everything else inside the crib, including herself. Her paint of choice came from a nearby source: the inside of her diaper.

She first surprised me with a sample of her talent one afternoon after she had taken what I thought to be an exceptionally long nap. I foolishly assumed, because no sound was coming from the bedroom, that my sweet baby had finally learned the art of sleeping. I was right about the "art" part. But it had nothing to do with sleeping. When I didn't hear the usual wake-up howl after a considerable amount of time, I became concerned. Getting up from the couch where I'd been enjoying a much-needed rest, I walked down the hall to the bedroom and opened the door.

"Oh, no!" I shrieked.

There, in her crib, smeared from head to toe in personal diaper deposits, sat Christina. Wearing a wide toothless grin, she peered at me through her poop-coated crib-bars, quite oblivious to the pungent mess she had made around her. After my initial shock, I approached her cautiously. Holding my breath to keep the stench at bay, I reached down and snapped her up, causing a few overlooked pebbles from inside her diaper to roll out onto the floor. Holding her at arm's length, we scurried off to the bathroom.

Cleanup was excruciating. My little artist had managed to weave her potty-wares into her hair, nose, and mouth. Picasso, himself, could not have done a better job.

Christina peaked at nonsleep at around the age of eleven months. Still waking for her nightly refill, she'd make her request, or rather, demand, by flinging her bottle out of the crib and onto the floor where it would land with a loud thump. This thump would, in turn, awaken the sleeping giant downstairs—our landlord, who slept with a thumper of his own, a broom. As sure as night follows day, three loud consecutive thumps would be heard after Christina's initial one. This was my cue to leap from the warmth of my covers and run wildly into the kitchen to fill another bottle, then run wildly back with it before Christina's lung power kicked in.

Sometimes I made it. Sometimes I didn't.

Once again, I would recall my mother telling me, "What doesn't kill you makes you stronger."

I grew mightier every day.

By the time Christina's first birthday rolled around, I realized I wasn't the same person I'd been before giving birth—or, as I referred to it, "Nancy, B.C." (before Christina). For one thing, I no longer took sleep for granted; it had become a sacred luxury that, if I was lucky, I could indulge in now and then.

I also learned to appreciate the joy of eating a meal without any interruptions. A long, private bath was now seen as a gift from heaven. In essence, I had learned how to cherish the little things. I had also learned to lower my expectations. (A lesson I would relearn repeatedly throughout the coming years.)

So, as Christina celebrated her first birthday, I celebrated my first birthday as a mother. Together, we had made it through the first experimental twelve months and survived.

I sat watching with pride as my laughing, bright-eyed, beautiful daughter, with chocolate icing smeared all over her face, sat happily in her high chair enjoying her first birthday cake. Somehow, the sleepless nights, hectic days, worries, and fears no longer seemed important. Only the joyful smile on Christina's face mattered. I wanted to see it forever . . . or at least until I had finished my piece of cake.

Nancy Ilk

Maternity Revisited

It was mid-January, mere weeks before the birth of our first child, when a friend camped out in the soon-to-be nursery for several days. Living just a few kilometers outside of Paris, we regularly enjoyed visits by friends from around the world who were drawn to the City of Lights.

Upon her departure, my friend left a sweet thank-you note on a card she'd picked up at the Picasso Museum. She had aptly chosen a print of his painting *Maternity*, which depicts a woman breastfeeding. The woman sits serenely, draped in a sheer, shimmering pink gown with a floral print, the gown sliding ever so sensuously off her left shoulder. Her slender neck slopes to the right as she gazes lovingly, dreamily down at her nursing infant. Her skin is flawless, her rosy lips slanted into a slight, relaxed smile. Her eyebrows are perfectly tweezed and arched across her creaseless forehead. Her silky brown hair is casually, but elegantly, pinned high on the back of her head with a fresh blossom, and the curling tendrils caress her neck on one side. She wears a blue stone ring on one hand, cradling the infant's head. The baby lies contentedly, swathed in folds of its mother's gown, one hand resting sweetly in her cleavage. It is a beautiful painting.

The picture evoked all that was maternal in me. Every time I neared my refrigerator, which I assure you was often in my ninth month of pregnancy, I would instinctually caress my bulging belly. My anticipation was great. Nursing my infant would call forth all feminine beauty and bring peace to my body and soul. Picasso said so.

Surprisingly, in the days and weeks following my son's birth, my response to the small card on my refrigerator began to change—rather drastically. The first few days home I was too dazed to notice anything as I stumbled through the house. When I did manage to focus in the direction of the painting one afternoon, a small pathetic sigh escaped my lips. The next time, I rolled my eyes. Eventually, I was scoffing and snorting my way through the kitchen.

As the days passed I felt irritation and antagonism rise within me at the sight of what's-her-name on the fridge. One evening while I paced the hallway, screaming infant in my arms, my husband stood looking on, debating whether to question why I was chanting, "I hate Picasso. I hate Picasso. I hate Picasso. . . ." Then, chalking it up to hormones, he quietly slunk away to watch a late show on TV.

I had been duped. I just wasn't experiencing that peace-and-beauty thing. The fact that there are piles of books—entire books!—written on breastfeeding, not to mention seminars, classes, counselors, lactation experts, and a worldwide La Leche League, should have tipped me off that Picasso didn't know what the hell he was painting about. The fact that he's a man might have at least brought a moment's hesitation. But I was idealistic and naive. I wanted to believe Picasso.

I considered a lawsuit: false advertising or some such thing. But to make my frustration complete, Picasso died a long time ago. Still, I felt a rebuttal of some kind must be launched. The idea hit me while I was wandering the halls at four in the morning. Another painting! In fact, I would have my own portrait done. I, with the help of some talented young artist up at Montmartre, would set the record straight. We would title the painting *Maternity Revisited* or maybe *Picasso Unplugged* or perhaps *Plugging Picasso.*

Anyway, the to-be-titled painting depicts me on my couch, surrounded by unfolded laundry with a plate from last night's frozen pizza at my elbow. I sit draped in my husband's blue flannel shirt—the same one I've worn for the past three days. It is buttoned unevenly and generously adorned over the collar, across the shoulders, and down the front with patterns of regurgitated milk.

I'm sitting on a pillow. Let's not talk about why. I have on sweat pants—the only thing I can find that fits. After nearly ten minutes of shark-like thrashing while I tried to shove a dripping nipple into his mouth, Levi managed to latch on. Every vein and tendon in my neck is taut, and my teeth are clenched against the agony of engorged breasts and cracked nipples. My lips are pursed for Lamaze breathing. A tear rolls down my left cheek.

Dark circles under bleary eyes tell of sleepless nights. I don't care about my eyebrows. They're not tweezed and probably never will be again. Like I need more pain? My skin is a mottled patchwork of spots that look like dirt or, more likely, smudges of chocolate. It's the mask of pregnancy, described in the fine print of my pregnancy handbook. Look for the paragraph that starts out, "While estrogen causes most women's skin to take on a healthy glow . . . blah, blah, blah."

My hair, difficult to describe, just might start a new trend in Paris. Suffice it to say that my hairbrush has been lost for days and is probably buried somewhere inside the couch. Lines of worry crease my brow—worry that my baby isn't getting enough milk, that my baby never sleeps, that he isn't getting enough milk, that my baby's skin is flaky, that he isn't getting enough milk, that my baby's poop looks funny, that he isn't getting enough milk, that my baby isn't breathing, that I'm sure he's not getting enough milk.

On the table beside me is the phone, which is guaranteed to ring as soon as I sit down to nurse, and a glass of water, which all the books say I need but which is just out of reach.

Rings? Forget it—my fingers have been too fat since my fifth month. My baby lies across his Boppy nursing pillow, side by side with a jealous Yorkshire terrier who is not taking kindly to giving up any lap space. As an older sibling, her regressive behavior is displayed in the carpet stains at my feet. A lacy white yarmulke—my nursing pad—sits on my son's head. It's the only place I seem to be able to keep track of it. His sweet little hand rests in my cleavage, occasionally kneading my tender flesh with his tiny razor fingernails.

I regard the finished painting. I feel strong emotion rising in my chest, only to realize that it's my milk coming in. Never mind. And never mind that I've been unable to arouse the slightest interest from even a single gallery in Paris. Fine. Fame and fortune are never the goal of true artists, anyway. Like so many great paintings, this one is obviously just ahead of its time. Let's face it, truth is not always pretty.

The important thing is I have made my peace with Picasso. In fact, my son has recently begun sleeping through the night, and I am suddenly at peace with the entire universe at large. Yesterday, I became one of those envied women who casually attaches baby to breast in public without raising a single eyebrow or missing a beat of conversation. Today, I am wearing a clean blouse and even a little mascara. And last evening, while dozing against the headboard during the 10:00 P.M. feeding, I startled awake to find my husband staring at me with a look I thought was gone for good.

"Maternity" is still hanging on my refrigerator. Over the past weeks I've devised various methods of destroying her, but now I'm glad I didn't. She and I have achieved solidarity. I'm feeling much less unplugged these days, and I am happy for any mothering inspiration. The peace and beauty thing kicked in; I'm peaceful and my son is a breathtaking beauty. He's showing all the signs of being exceptionally bright and creative. Perhaps he'll be a painter.

Kristi Hemingway

Beware of Shifting Tides

Everyone who meets my husband thinks he's great. His kind, gentle, and relaxed demeanor is a perfect match for me—someone who seems as if she's made one too many trips to Starbucks. When I became pregnant, it added a new dimension to our yin-yang personalities.

Like many expectant couples, we attended Lamaze classes. One evening as I lay on the floor of the class practicing a new relaxation technique, I heard the instructor say, "Everybody, look at Sharon." Excited that I was being used as the class example, I tried to stay still.

"Can you all see how tense she is?" the instructor said.

What? Tense?

The class laughed. My husband laughed the loudest. Although I should have felt angry at his laughter, it actually made me feel more relaxed. At that moment, I knew I would need him by my side during the throes of childbirth.

Yet, on that humid August day as we drove to the hospital, filled with anticipation about the miracle that was about to happen, my enraged hormones had other ideas about Bill's presence in the delivery room. Women are known to experience varying degrees of hormonal personality changes regularly, but on a scale of one to ten, mine easily spikes once a month to about a 9.5—a great score if I were an Olympic gymnast, not so great for a wife. Pregnancy was no exception. According to my husband, it did not bring out my most delightful side. And that morning, as my body kicked into baby-delivery mode, the hormonal swing was dramatic.

Still, my dedicated husband stood by my side and coached me to help ease my pain.

Taking my hand in his, he asked, "Do you feel comfortable?"

"I'm fine," I replied a bit curtly.

A short while later, "Do you need any ice chips?"

I gritted my teeth and counted to five before I answered. "No thanks."

"Can I get you a damp washcloth for your forehead?"

"Are we playing twenty questions?" I shouted at him.

Now, logically, I knew these were all fair questions. In fact, they were downright supportive. But inside I felt an irritation . . . an irritation at his very presence.

Be nice, I told myself. With a forced a smile, I said, "I'm sorry. I'll let you know if I need anything."

The labor pains continued throughout the morning. With each pain, my husband would run to my side to assist me through the breathing, which, for some reason, infuriated me.

When the nurse entered the room and my husband stepped aside, I noticed my level of annoyance drop. My anger seemed to fester only towards him.

After almost four long hours of everyone, including my husband, saying "push," I finally delivered our baby daughter. My tongue was held firmly in place by the "good angel" that sat on my shoulder, who whispered in my ear throughout the entire ordeal that my husband is a good man.

Four of us left the hospital a few days later: Bill, me, and our new baby were stalked by my enraged hormones, which followed us out the door and into our car. And in the weeks and months that followed, they trailed behind me everywhere I went. Unexplained weepiness, unexplained anger, even unexplained bliss! Sadly, most of my wrath was directed toward my sweet spouse.

One afternoon as we drove home from an errand, he mentioned some thoughts he had about a project we had considered for our home. Slyly, I looked at him out of the corner of my eye. Everything he said sounded insane. *What is wrong with him?* I thought.

It was sad to feel this way. I wondered if I'd ever feel "normal" again. This man was the love of my life; in fact, I loved him more than anything . . . right up until the moment we entered that stupid hospital.

Several months later, after one too many afternoons of breastmilk spots appearing without warning on my shirt, I made the decision to stop breastfeeding. Within forty-eight hours, my body returned to a normal state. To my surprise, the ongoing hormonal shifts had been directly related to my body's milk production.

The dark cloud that had hovered over me for many long months lifted. I felt like a new woman. My husband appeared before me through new eyes. Light illuminated around him. Well, perhaps that is a slight exaggeration, but he looked so wonderful to me, it might as well have.

It was hard for me to believe that my hormones could wreak such havoc. As we approached the birth of our second child, I worried about what to expect during the delivery. At least we'd both know the reason behind my wrath if my fangs came out this time.

I'm happy to report that on our second trip to the delivery room, the only person I needed throughout the entire ordeal was my husband. His love and support carried me through the day. Even through another four hours of pushing, I loved him more than ever.

And this time, when we were discharged from the hospital, only three of us left: Bill, me, and our second baby girl. The hormonal stalkers never emerged.

Tidal changes are easily determined by the moon's rotation around the earth. But any good sailor would tell you that the tidal shifts can vary based on many factors. Navigating through life can be difficult, too. I never know which way the tides in my life will shift, but when they do, I try to keep the faith, stay the course, and sail right through them.

Sharon A. Struth

And I Pray for Baby Ike

One particular picture tells the story best. It was taken the day we brought my youngest son, Ike, home from the hospital. We are all sitting on the couch in our living room. I'm holding the baby; next to me is my husband, and next to him is Sam, my older son, leaning on his dad's shoulder. The look on Sam's face is full of gloom.

It is a far cry from the smiles and laughs that are in the pictures of Sam hovering over his new brother, Ike, in the hospital only a day earlier. In those pictures, Sam is wearing a surgical mask that a nurse friend had given him. Dressed up like a little doctor, Sam blows kisses through the mask to his new sibling, who is sleeping in his bassinet. It is obvious that Sam is enthralled with Ike. While we were in the hospital, Sam asked us all the questions he could possibly think of about our new family member and even brought us flowers with smiley faces glued to them "to make Ike laugh."

But the other picture tells the story of how things went once we got home. Sam, who was four at the time, lurked in the corner while Ike in his little carrier crossed the door to our house. When Sam saw us, he stayed far away from the spectacle. He had spent the morning making snowmen in the front yard with my parents to welcome us home. I told him they looked great, but he just shrugged his shoulders. And, as we started to settle in, my mother took the picture of us on the couch. Minutes after it was taken, I heard Sam ask, "When is he going back?"

That night, after the baby was asleep, I went into Sam's room. I knew it was cliché, but suddenly I felt like I was looking at a different child. He was bigger. He was older. He was wiser than I remembered. And, as he looked up at me, I knew he was wondering how much his life was going to change now that little Ike was a part of it.

"Let's say your prayers, okay?" I said.

He rolled his back to me.

"It will be all right," I told him, placing my hand on his shoulder. "Let's say them together."

So we said his prayers and, as was tradition, Sam ended his prayer with his list of special people he wanted God to look out for that night. He prayed for me and his dad. He prayed for his grandparents. He prayed for his friends. He prayed for the cat.

In the silence that followed, I whispered to Sam that he forgot to add someone to his prayer list.

He looked up at me, confused, "Who?"

I gently reminded him about his new brother. "We prayed for him when he was in my belly."

Sam let out a long sigh. "Okay." He quickly added to the end of his prayer, "And I pray for baby Ike."

Because of the four-year age difference between my sons, I knew it would take some time for them to develop much of a relationship. And, although I had hoped for the immediate affection that some friends had shared with me that their children had for the new baby from birth, I was willing to give Sam the time and space he needed to show his love for his brother.

And it took some time.

The situation was not helped by the fact that Ike was a high-needs baby. There were many times when Sam was trapped with us in the car while Ike endlessly wailed on our way to somewhere, and there were many times when I had to give my attention to Ike over Sam because, well, he was a baby.

For at least the first year, Sam treated Ike with indifference. Sam knew Ike was part of our family, but he still couldn't figure out what Ike's role was in the family. I worried that the boys wouldn't bond and that we were setting the record for the longest time for a sibling to accept a new brother. All of the pregnancy books had made it sound like the trip from gloomy to rosy could take a while, but "a while" was a matter of months according to their advice.

So, much to my dismay, Ike stayed at the end of Sam's nightly prayers . . . after the cat.

It wasn't as though Sam was mean to Ike. He just seemed uninterested in his little brother. That was, until Ike started getting into Sam's stuff. Then battles would ensue and doors were locked. Somehow, Ike had radar for the "stuff" that was important. He would zero in on it and destroy Sam's special object in a matter of seconds.

Then Ike turned two. And just when I thought things were going to get worse between them, something unexpected happened.

One day, as I drove Sam home from school with Ike sitting next to him in his car seat, I told Sam about our day and our visit to the local playgroup. "And poor Ike got that nasty bump because another kid ran right into him," I said as we got out of the car to go into the house.

Sam stopped in his tracks. "What happened?"

"Oh, a little kid ran right into him and knocked him down."

"He knocked him down?" Sam looked up at me. "Someone knocked down my little brother. Who was it?"

I tried to hide my smile when I looked down at Sam. His chest was all puffed up and his face was red. He looked ready to rumble. "Don't worry, honey, he's fine. It was just an accident."

"Oh," said Sam. "I thought someone was trying to hurt Ike. I would not like that at all."

He finished walking up the stairs into the house and waited at the top to make sure his brother made it in the door.

From that moment on, things seemed to slowly change. Maybe they had been in motion for some time up to that point, but it was now apparent to me that something was starting to happen.

As Ike's language slowly developed, Sam started asking him questions and actually waited for an answer. When the pillows got pulled off the couches, Sam would invite Ike into his new fort to bounce. And when bedtime rolled around, they loved to crawl into Sam's bed to listen to stories.

My heart skips when I see them together. They run the same way—their feet slightly turned out, their arms low to their sides. Sometimes, it is all I can do not to cry when I watch Sam help Ike into his chair or read him a book.

I do dream that my boys will become wonderful friends. I want them to develop the bond now that will last them a lifetime. At the ages of six and two, it's hard to know how everything will turn out, but for now, it's nice to hear Ike move up in the ranks. Because at night when it's time for prayers, the list has not changed, but the placement has; it usually goes Mom, Dad, Ike . . . and then the cat.

Janine Boldrin

I'm Having a Baby . . . Really!

I'm having a baby.

Not that you would know it to look at me. My stomach, while not exactly flat, lacks that telltale baby bulge. But I am having a baby. I just don't know when.

My husband and I are adopting, and while the physical symptoms of pregnancy may be absent, the reality that we're going to be parents is beginning to set in. We're talking about names, looking at cribs, and admiring tiny little onesies in gender-neutral shades.

But as we examine car seats and strollers and changing tables, I find I feel like an imposter. I don't have the burgeoning belly or giveaway glow that the other future mommies do. Our child isn't growing inside me. We don't even know when to expect her or him. We just know a baby is coming.

Erik and I have endured years of well-meaning questions about whether we want kids. Well, yeah. A couple of years of trying the old-fashioned way led to fertility drugs, surgeries, and interventions that eventually culminated in five rounds of in vitro. I did manage to get pregnant several times, only to miscarry every time. During that six years, we withdrew from the world. Only our closest friends knew what we were going through, but even they couldn't understand the pain we were experiencing. Why I couldn't go to a baby shower. Why I pointedly ignored pregnant women anywhere I saw them. Why I couldn't bear to even look at a baby.

Over time, my hope to carry a biological child began to dim. But my desire to be a mommy grew stronger. For most people, pregnancy and parenthood are irretrievably linked. Others realize that giving up one needn't negate the other. I'll never carry a child or see my belly swell or feed my baby at my breast. But is that really what being a parent is about? I believe not.

So I gave up my pregnancy fantasy and focused on becoming a mom. My husband and I met with social workers, filled out reams of paperwork, and took a ten-week parenting class. We were fingerprinted, our backgrounds checked, our mental and physical health examined, and our house inspected.

We spent hours writing a "dear birth parents" letter, trying to put into words our desire to be parents, choosing photos that reflect our responsible yet fun-loving selves, and promising our love, time, and attention along with baby swim classes and homemade chocolate chip cookies. We started advertising. We received our license to adopt. And then we waited.

Our baby could be born any day! We knew it could happen that fast. But I couldn't share our excitement with the world. There was no steadily growing stomach, no due date to circle on the calendar. After trying to have a baby for so many years, now we really were . . . and yet our baby felt like a secret. We weren't able to share our joy with everyone we knew and met.

While at a conference out of town, I realized people couldn't, and wouldn't, know we were "expecting" a baby unless we told them. So I started spreading the news. I announced to long-distance friends I saw only once a year at this event, "I have big news. I'm going to be a mom!" I told business colleagues at the conference. Then I told anyone who would listen.

And people were thrilled. They congratulated, hugged, and blessed me. I met moms, dads, aunts, and grandpas who had adopted children. I met adopted adults who told me how happy they were for me. With each good wish and each kind word, my baby became more real. But I didn't realize how healing the joy of sharing my big news was until I got on the plane to return home.

The man sitting directly behind me was holding a newborn—six weeks, I overheard him say. When I got up to go to the restroom, I looked at the infant. For the first time in years, I could look at a baby. I could admire his tiny body, his feathery eyelashes, his rosebud mouth, and his loosely clenched fingers without feeling that awful mix of desire, jealousy, and sorrow. I gazed at this precious little person, sleeping so peacefully, and was no longer reminded of what I had lost or would never have. Instead, I saw hope and joy—and certainty. Instead, I thought, *I'm getting one of those!*

"He's beautiful," I told the baby's father, who looked up at me and smiled. And our baby will be too.

Kelly James-Enger

Kelly James-Enger met her son, Ryan, a few weeks after writing this essay. He's just as beautiful as she thought he'd be.

This story was first published in Chicago Parent, *November 2006.*

The Night and the New Mom

My alarm sounds, and I reach over to shut it off. The time reads 3:15 A.M., and I'm already wide awake. I've been awake, in fact, for the past ten minutes, my body tense, listening to Aidan breathing in the Pack 'n Play. He breathes loudly, like Darth Vader. Is this normal? Does he have gas? Is he okay? The only thing keeping me in place, one ear tipped in his direction, is the knowledge that at least he's alive.

Though I've been in bed for the last three hours, I've slept lightly, jolted awake by the smallest of noises from my baby. A few minutes ago, Aidan started to stir, grunting like a piglet. I've been waiting for the alarm. Waiting to rise, take him in my arms, and trudge down the hallway to the living room, where it's brighter, to feed him. In the bedroom, we have heavy blinds to block out Alaska's midnight sun. But a few feet past the bedroom door, I will be able to see my baby's face clearly.

As I push back the sheets, I look enviously at my husband—the lump beneath the comforter next to me, so snug in dreamland. Motherhood's weight of responsibility has hit me, and at night, it's that much heavier. Because it's late. And I'm alone. And because of the uncertainty, the doubts regarding my ability as a new mom. I am a confused, tired mess, and I'm terrified that something will happen to my child. Especially at night.

I give a final glance in my husband's direction. He hasn't budged. Surely, he's heard Aidan? But he gives no sign of it. He's peaceful. Asleep. And I accept it because this is our agreement. I pump and feed—or try to nurse—and he sleeps. No use both of us being exhausted. But for the next hour, at least, I will be on my own. Caring for a tiny human being. I, a new mom, with no prior baby skills. Going on nothing but instinct and a few weeks of experience. Feeling the effects of extreme sleep-deprivation and not completely coherent. I, a teacher used to teenagers, not infants, now responsible for changing, feeding, and clothing a squirmy, needy, sometimes unhappy little person. One who can't explain what he wants, who requires sterilized feeding equipment, and who makes an enormous amount of noise if he doesn't get what he wants quickly enough. I have to perform these duties expertly, in the middle of the night. The situation terrifies me.

I struggle out of bed, my breasts heavy and sore and dripping milk, and bend down to pick up my now fully awake, half-swaddled baby. How he always manages to free his arms is beyond me. I carry him down the hall and into the kitchen to warm a bottle of breastmilk with Aidan tucked close to my chest. Everything in the house is quiet. The windows are open, and the cool Alaska air circulates the smells of Pampers, milk, and everything baby. It's the end of a swelteringly hot July, and even at this time of night, there's no need to flick on a light switch.

Aidan's getting heavy, and I'm having a hard time holding him and warming the milk at the same time. His eyes are also opening wider with all the jostling, so I hurry into the living room and place him on a blanket. Then I dash back into the kitchen to run the hot water in the sink. He grunts in the next room, and I hurry back. Crouching on the floor, I unswaddle him and change his diaper. My back aches, and I think how happy I will be once we buy Aidan a changing table and crib. Diaper changed, I dart back into the kitchen and grab the now luke-warm milk along with the tape and feeding tube.

Breastfeeding has caused such toe-curling pain that I rarely attempt it at night. Instead, I use this makeshift device: one end of a tiny tube is inserted into the nipple of a bottle while the other end is taped to my forefinger. With Aidan supported in my lap, I place my finger in his mouth and let him suck, trying not to stare at the clock that now reads 3:35 or to think about everyone in Fairbanks who is asleep. Except me. And, of course, Aidan.

Let's be honest. As a kid, waking in the middle of the night was scary. You couldn't see where you were going. Your parents (i.e., your protectors) were asleep. And, as anybody would tell you, only bad people were out, cruising streets or lurking in bushes. If absolutely necessary, you hurried on tip-toe to the bathroom, did your business, and rushed back to the safety of your covers as fast as possible.

As an adult, nighttime wakings have brought me similar feelings of tentativeness and apprehension. Who likes to be awakened out of a dead sleep? The mind is foggy, the house is so still you can hear it settling, and all sane people are asleep. Irrationally, I think that if anyone were to, say, enter the house and attack me, there'd be no one to help.

Having a newborn has brought me face-to-face with these middle-of-the-night fears. At first, the night was unknown. Semi-dark, still, quiet. A stranger I didn't want to know.

On the couch, I continue to finger-feed Aidan, waiting for him to suck up all the milk so I can burp him, pump, and get back in bed. But after a while, as I watch him drink, my muscles relax, my mind wanders, and I think less about the night and more about my son. What a miracle he is. What a perfect, beautiful gift. *I have company in the middle of the night*, I think, finally. *This isn't that bad.* Wordlessly, effortlessly, my son has become my comfort.

"My sweet son," I say, sliding my finger out of his mouth, the bottle now dry. His eyelids hang heavily over his blue eyes, and relief spreads across his face. Mmmm, milk. He smacks his lips, curls into himself. He's limp and newly sleepy. I pat his back, holding him close to my heart. Aidan's body is warm against mine. He needs me, and suddenly I realize I need him too.

With the feeding done, I decide that I'm not ready to put him back in his Pack 'n Play. Not ready to pump and to be alone again. Instead, I carry Aidan to the broad bay window. Together, we look into the empty street, at the shadows beneath our car and the faint puddles of light under the street lamps. The aspen's leaves rustle in the night breeze. I inhale the sweet northern air, the woodsy scent of all that is Alaska. The sun hovers just below the horizon, but houses remain dark, their inhabitants asleep. I hold my baby close.

Then, out of nowhere, a black cat appears, stealing up the driveway. Its sleek back undulates under its coat as it stalks some unseen rodent.

"Aidan, look!" I whisper. "Mee-ow." I point and we stare. Except, Aidan's blue eyes are turned on me. The cat continues its hunt, and now I'm gazing at my little boy in the twilight. Together, the two of us, awake in the night. His bare skin—arms, face, hands, and legs—against me. The two of us. Together.

Though tired—no, exhausted—I'm not ready to carry him back down the hall yet. We've just seen a cat together! Just my baby and me. No one else in the world shared this experience with us. At once, I'm exhilarated. *I can do this*, I think. *This mothering thing. Even in the middle of the night.*

Over the next few weeks, the night slowly becomes our friend. Together, Aidan and I share time in the night. Getting to know each other without the bustle of parents and in-laws, friends, or even my husband. With the comfort of the night air and the quietness of the night, I'm also free to think. To let my mind wander. Free to become the mother I want to be to my son. The bright Alaskan days seem so much busier with a constant reminder of what I can't get done. Cleaning? Too tired. Walks? Too sore. Writing? Too stressful. The night puts no pressure on me. I am awake for one reason only: to care for—and enjoy—my son.

During the day, I play several roles. Hostess to my in-laws. Companion to my husband. Conversationalist to friends. With Aidan's birth, I'm in this new role of "mother," expected to know how to change a diaper, bathe and dress the baby, nurse the baby, and play with the baby. Sometimes I get stressed when there's too much going on at once (and too many pairs of eyes watching!). I don't know how, exactly, to play with a newborn, and frankly, I often don't have the energy. If he's fed and his diaper is clean, I want to rest. Or check my e-mail. Or eat. And I don't necessarily want someone else to take over with my baby. Because I'm the mom. And really, I can do this.

The days are also noisy. With questions and talk. With TV and music. With the neighbor's children playing in the yard. Cars racing up and down the street. Too much. All those sunny hours with others are tough.

But the night. Ah, the quiet night is different. It puts me in charge, with no one else offering advice or needing my hospitality. Despite how scary the sole responsibility of an infant is, the benefits gradually overcome the drawbacks. The night gives me a break from being "on" with the in-laws and super-nice with friends who stay way too long. With everyone else asleep, I grow as a mother, the real mother inside me. I don't have anyone saying, "Want me to hold him?" or "I disagree with you about tummy time." At night, I don't have to please anyone but my baby and myself. The night liberates me. It gives me peace. It becomes something I look forward to.

Aidan is now eight months old and sleeping through the night more and more frequently. As much as I love seven or eight consecutive hours of sleep, there's a part of me that misses those nighttime feedings. That hour when he cries out for me. Me. To feed him at the breast (finally!). To comfort and soothe him. It's our quiet time together. It's when the moon cuts through the darkness, allowing me to see his face. Satisfied, with a full belly. Smiling, because he's happy I'm there.

After seeing the cat that night so many months ago, I swaddled Aidan—arms tucked tightly inside—and carried him back down the hall. I kissed his cheek, placed him in the Pack 'n Play, and returned to the kitchen to pump. It had become a little lonelier. But my chest still held the warmth of Aidan's body, and riding a high of baby love helped me get through the chore of eking milk into two bottles.

In the end, the night has been good to me. I may not have been the most rested mother during the day, but I never wished for our nightly rendezvous to stop. Because, during those few short first months, Aidan was, in the semi-darkness, mine and mine alone.

My son has grown in the night. And so have I.

Mary Jo Marcellus Wyse

Simply Perfect

"It's a boy!" cheers the midwife. A burly blond dad with a day-old beard, wearing a Stren Fishing Line T-shirt, swells with pride like an overinflated gym ball. A glowing young mother reclines in the birthing center bed cradling a plump newborn boy. Cut. Slow-motion shot of man embracing wife. "Honey, he's what I've always wanted. You're the best. I love you." Kiss. Cry.

Pop!

My bubble just burst.

"It's a girl!" cheered the midwife. The tiny pink girl cried. I cried. My husband, David, cried.

In a sacred voice David whispered, "She's perfect."

And she was. Our second child could be a boy.

Two years later, I unearthed the baby boy pajamas from my hope chest. I had buried them next to
a commemorative photo of Michael Jordan and my
college diploma.

"Should we name this baby David Junior?" I
quizzed my husband. My belly, a bowling ball, bulged
over the kitchen sink as I washed dishes.

No response from David. He was busy coaching
our little girl. "Hands like this . . . there . . . now,
look at the rim and shoot! Nice shot, sweetie!" His
strong frame folded down to our daughter, embracing
her.

Our boy would resemble his dad: blond, blue-
eyed, quick to smile. Captain of the basketball team.
Voted nicest hair in high school . . .

"It's a girl!" cheered the midwife.

Wow. Another one. What are the chances? Like,
fifty-fifty? I never considered another girl. Dave's boy,
he'd come next time. "Right, Dave? . . . Dave?"

But David was lost in his two-minute-old daughter, pressing her close, tears of awe drizzling down his
unshaven face. "She's perfect," he cooed.

I devoured books on gender selection: Avoid
tomatoes and acidic foods. Timing is important. So

is position. Arrange bed so your head points north
. . .

I forced a slanted smile when unsolicited advice
flew my way. "Whoever wears the pants in the family
determines the baby's gender," snickered a grocery
store check-out lady.

"You want boys?" hacked out an eighty-year-old
church lady chasing me down the aisle of the sanctuary. She had hearing loss and eight sons. "Orgasm!
Orgasm! Orgasm!"

This gender-selection thing was beginning to
sound a little like an infomercial for a kitchen appli-
ance: "Fast! Simple! Fun, too!"

Over the next six years I dug up the baby boy
pajamas three more times. I gave birth to three more
girls.

"It's a girl!" cheered the midwife each time.

"I thought so," I sighed each time. "We're running out of girls' names."

"She's perfect," David professed each time.

Our all-of-a-kind family was beautiful. I loved our
girls. Each one. But something unfamiliar gnawed at
the edges of my heart. Was it despair? Don't get me
wrong; I liked girls. I was once a girl myself. But
David—his plans, his dreams, his son . . .

Then one May morning while clearing the
breakfast dishes, I glanced out our kitchen window.

Five flowering crabapple trees, one for each child, wore ringlets of delicate pink blossoms. Five little girls played together in the back yard. Two of our girls played catch with a football. Our blond-haired, blue-eyed, daddy-look-alike daughter sat beside a pink Huffy repairing a loose handlebar. Who taught her to use a wrench? Our fourth daughter squatted near the untilled garden, digging in the cold black soil for earthworms. And the fifth, our newest baby girl, cried as David placed her in the grass. "Da-da! Da-da!" she squealed, arms outstretched. He picked her up.

The morning sun illuminated the scene, framing my family: My husband. My girls. My . . . boy. How could I have not seen it before? These little girls are what David has wanted. He wanted a family. He was content. I was the one who wanted a son. A boy was my desire, my ache. Not his.

That morning in my kitchen I said aloud to my refrigerator, my toaster, and my sink, "I want a boy!" There was no rationale. A son would not bring status or wealth or security to our family. Nothing was "missing" from our family. I didn't want a son for my husband. I didn't want a son for me. I wanted a son for some reason outside of reason. Somewhere my soul said, "I want a son," and I didn't know why.

Two years later I lifted the lid on my hope chest again. As I rummaged through my past for the baby boy pajamas, I stopped. Shut the top. Went away. And gave birth . . . to a boy.

We didn't name our son David Junior. Andrew—that's his name—is topped with a swatch of brown hair. He has dark eyes, dark skin. He looks like me. He may one day play ball, fish, and coach like his dad. Or he may one day dance, sing, and write like his mom.

My son will never wear the baby boy pajamas. They're kept deep in my hope chest. Someday, in the distant future, when my children—my girls or my boy—struggle with something their souls cannot explain, I'll pull out the baby boy pajamas and tell them, "I once wanted something, too. I didn't know why. It looked impossible. But now I have five perfect daughters . . . and one perfect, soul-sent son."

Cristy Trandahl

All New Mommies See Double

When my firstborn son arrived, I didn't tell anyone I'd wished for a girl. By the time his brother was born, two and a half years after that, I stopped hoping altogether. By then, I swapped baby stories like a pro: New moms can't wait to fit into their skinny jeans again. Some days, we're lucky to get ourselves dressed, much less the baby. New moms are so tired from getting up for 2:00 A.M. feedings that we walk into walls . . .

Six years later, I'd forgotten what having a baby was like. Besides, with the two boys, my husband and I felt our family was complete. True, I'd wanted a girl, but things hadn't turned out that way, and two boys were plenty. Many infertile couples would be grateful for one healthy child.

Just before we relocated to Oregon, I began to have stomach troubles. By Halloween, I had to force my weary, nauseated self to sit behind the teacher's desk in my third-grade class. To keep my lunch down, I nibbled on Saltines. I hadn't felt so tired since . . . wait. These symptoms sounded familiar. I couldn't *really* be pregnant. Could I?

A home pregnancy test confirmed my suspicions. I told my husband, opening with, "You're not gonna believe this, but . . ."

After I revived him, he smiled, faintly. Very faintly.

My moods shifted by the hour, from mild disappointment to eager anticipation and back again. At times I couldn't imagine myself going through pregnancy, labor, delivery, and breastfeeding. Gradually, though, the news sank in. I was going to be a new mother. Again. In mid-June.

I'd thought I was finished with the crib, so I'd donated it. Our garage was still piled high with two different styles of strollers, a high chair stained with spaghetti sauce, an old play pen, and a diaper duck. But I'd thrown out some of the mountain of stuff one accumulates along with a new baby, like the diaper bag and ultrasoft hairbrush, and I'd given away most of the rest—the swing and car seats, the nose syringe and teensy nail clippers, the receiving blankets and crib sheets, the booties and those little mitts that keep babies from scratching themselves, and whatever onesies, sleepers, and other clothing that wasn't so stained and worn out that nobody would dare put them on their child.

Of course, it was too soon to start shopping for baby things. Besides, we'd be moving to Oregon in a few months and didn't want to move anything more than we already had to. Nevertheless, I dragged my sons through the girls' department of clothing and department stores. I'd finger lacy dresses and ooh and ah over pink and purple outfits. My boys let me know how they felt. "Eeeww," they'd chime, holding their noses, "stinky girl stuff." I'd scold myself, too: *This might not be a girl. And that would be fine. I'd be fine with another boy. Three healthy sons would be just fine.*

Still, while buying Matchbox cars or shirts teeming with dinosaurs, I'd daydream about hair ribbons and Barbie dolls.

Bumping up Interstate 5 from California to Oregon in a rental van, I felt tired and sick and old. For an expectant "new" mother, I felt really, really old. Big, too. At only four months along, I looked like I had at six months with my previous two pregnancies. I didn't remember getting that beached whale look quite so soon. By mid-June, they'd have to wheel me to the hospital on one of those extra-large carts from Costco . . . if I survived that long.

Despite my misery during the drive, we arrived safely in Oregon, where everything is wet and green, and moved into a small, two-bedroom house. The boys whooped and hollered and played in the February rain, which turned to slushy snow. I whooped, too, but my hollers were about the sugar-ant-infested kitchen and the fact that there was only a small wood stove for heat. The garage was piled high with logs. Since my husband was leaving straightaway for a temporary job in another city, I'd be chopping wood to keep us from freezing to death.

I put on my best Girl Scout face and a ratty, extra-large flannel shirt and got to work on the kindling. Meanwhile, the dear unborn child I carried practiced a few chops of its own, mostly to my kidneys.

I visited a doctor, who measured my abdomen and told me my calculations were off by at least a month. "You're due in May, not June," he said.

"I've never been wrong before," I huffed.

The doctor wasn't convinced. "Plan on May seventeenth," he said.

On the way home from the appointment, I couldn't decide what I hated most: Oregon rain, my swollen ankles, or my growing conviction that I was going to deliver another male addition to our budding basketball team.

I was in the kitchen fighting off the insect invasion when my husband got home. I cornered him, still wielding a broom and dustpan. "The boys keep tracking mud all over the carpet," I whined, brushing dead ants into the kitchen trash. "The doctor says I'm due in May instead of June." I held back tears. "And I can't stand this rain."

He put his arm around me. "You got rid of the ants, didn't you?"

I nodded.

He smiled. "Rain makes everything green." He leaned the broom and pan against the wall. "Besides, you're cute when you're pregnant, as cute as that University of Oregon mascot, Donald."

I cut him a scalding look. "Are you saying I walk like a duck?"

"I'm just saying you fit right in." He wisely fled into the garage to chop more wood.

Most of the time, though, he did everything right—massaged my back and made postmidnight ice cream runs. If I grumbled, he'd say, "Don't worry, honey, only two trimesters to go." I swear I was green only from morning sickness, not from pondering how long a trimester feels like when you can't see your feet.

By the eighth month, my stomach was the size of a small European country. I had more aches and pains than I remembered having with the first two. Every night, I set a new record for number of bathroom trips in an hour. My formerly innie belly button was so far out I thought it might explode. All those things were normal pregnancy complaints, but I was worried about something more serious. I adored the baby who kicked me in the bladder about a hundred times an hour, but I couldn't make peace with the thought of being the only female in a house full of males.

I was so sure we'd have another boy that I hadn't bothered to put together much of a nursery. A relative donated a rickety crib, an old bassinet, and a car seat, but I figured I'd just recycle the faded blue layette I'd saved. As the doctor's predicted May due date drew near, I became even crabbier, bigger, and more uncomfortable.

Then, one day, my oldest son laid his chubby first-grader's hand on my bloated belly and asked, "Mommy, are you having twins?"

Gulp. Sure, my wedding band was stuck on my swollen ring finger, I'd developed a raccoon-like pregnancy mask, and my baby bump was more like a large mountain chain. But twins? Was I really that huge? Or was I about to give birth to a giant?

Mid-May arrived. If I'd truly miscalculated and wasn't due in June, I was determined to get things moving. I walked the hills around my neighborhood until dark every evening. I toyed with the idea of drinking castor oil but couldn't bring myself to buy any. I made arrangements for the boys to stay with friends, but third-time expectant moms don't bother packing a suitcase until the last minute. I was an expert at having babies. Especially boy babies.

The weather became warmer and drier, and I wore T-shirts made for Big and Tall men. One day I waddled up and down the street, trying to picture my three sons playing, laughing, and growing together. *Maybe it won't be so bad,* I thought. *I'll probably enjoy being the Queen Bee.* As I puffed my way over a hill, my abdomen rose up, like a fist clenching. No pain, just a periodic tightening that lifted my whole tummy. How odd. But just like these painless movements, my attitude had changed. Now, I couldn't wait to meet my youngest son, the boy we'd call Timothy.

By that night, the tightenings were coming closer together. I felt slight pain, but nothing I couldn't handle. Perhaps I was so good at labor that I'd deliver my new son before midnight and be home by the next day. I casually mentioned all this to my husband. We called the doctor, dropped off the boys, and headed to the hospital.

Minutes later, I leaned back in the labor room bed while a nurse checked my dilation. My husband sat in a chair beside me.

"So it's Timothy Joel, right?" I said to him, in as relaxed a voice as anyone enduring the gloved finger test could be.

"That's the name I like best," he said.

The nurse piped up. "What if you have a girl? Do you have a girl's name picked out, too?"

My husband and I glanced at each other and smiled. He said, "We're pretty sure it's a boy."

The nurse looked surprised. "But what if it isn't? What then?"

A hard contraction began, and I quickly employed my Lamaze breathing. As it subsided, I whispered, "Okay. If it's a girl, we'll go with Alyssa Marie."

My husband nodded and squeezed my hand. I concentrated on the waves of pain that came and went, riding them like a drunk on a bicycle. As the night wore on, I resisted transitional urges to swear like a sailor and to bite anyone who came within range.

By seven in the morning, I was exhausted and so ready to push. A couple minutes later, the doctor finally showed up but allowed me to remain in the labor bed. I wasn't hooked up to a heart monitor, intravenous line, or any other instrument. Soft yellow light gave the room a comforting feel. Plus, in the labor room my husband could still watch television.

The doctor said I could bear down. With a few practiced pushes, I delivered my third child at 7:15 A.M.

The nurse said, "It's a girl!"

I gasped as she laid a swaddled Alyssa in my arms. I gazed up at my husband to share the magic moment. We finally had a daughter.

I glanced up, happy to be a mom—and my heart stopped. The doctor and nurse stood at the foot of the bed with horrified expressions on their faces. *What was wrong? Did Alyssa have all her fingers and toes?* Before I could tear off my daughter's blanket, the doctor yelled, "There's another one in there. And it's a boy!"

A nurse swept Alyssa away, and I was hastily prepped for a second delivery. Timothy Joel arrived seventeen minutes later, breach but without need for a cesarean section. Just like his sister, he was four to five weeks premature, beautiful, and completely unexpected.

My June due date had been correct, after all— the sheepish doctor hadn't even suspected twins and had never ordered an ultrasound to check. For days, his error was the talk of the maternity ward. After a short stay in the neonatal ICU, both babies came home healthy.

With time and effort, I managed to reduce to something close to my prepregnancy figure, although my ring fingers still sometimes swell and my jeans are often a bit snug. I certainly walked into walls for a time and didn't sleep through the night for years. I'll be a new mom seeing double for a long time to come, but our family is now complete.

Linda S. Clare

Labor of Love

At thirty-five and pregnant for the first time, I was given the illustrious title of "elderly prima gravida." Only in obstetrics is thirty-five considered elderly. Sure, I have a few strands of silver-white hair, but the fact that I still get pimples should exempt me from being called "elderly" anything. Still, as an elderly first-time mother, I approached pregnancy with all the prudence that such a moniker infers. We took a natural birthing class with a midwife and chose a hospital that respected birth plans and had wireless fetal monitors. I practiced Gaskin's sphincter law, did prenatal yoga, and to thwart an episiotomy, we did perineal massage. Right down to my birth plan, I was an obstetric pain in the ass. I knew what I wanted—a natural, vaginal, unmedicated birth. Thankfully, my husband was on board.

We photographed my growing stomach at every stage and always talked to our little "Bean," as we called him. My husband would put his head to my belly and say, "Beany, Beany, Beany, Beany. It's Daddy." Then he'd tell Bean about his day and how much we loved him already and were looking forward to meeting him, all while rubbing him gently.

Bean (Michael) was on board with the plan too, but not without giving Mama a little bit of grief before making his appearance. For several weeks before his estimated due date of February 5, 2006, we were in the first phase of stage-one labor. At 50 percent effaced, my cervix hovered between 1.5 and 2 centimeters dilated. I had strong, consistent, beyond–Braxton Hicks contractions that sent us to labor and delivery triage several times.

Michael was loving his hotel-womb a bit too much. His extended stay was only complicated by my suffering from the vestiges of a horrible cold, including a cough and laryngitis. February 5 came and went . . . but not without another visit to the L&D triage. Being elderly prima gravida, I was informed, "Oh, we won't let you go past a week. You'll be induced." And with that, an induction was tentatively scheduled for the following Sunday at 6:00 P.M. On one hand, I was thrilled to know that it wouldn't be much longer. On the other, I was not happy about

an induction, which meant Pitocin, probably an epidural, and a higher chance of a cesarean.

At my forty-one-week OB appointment, my cervix was 80 percent effaced and 2 centimeters dilated,
and Michael's head had moved to a plus-two station.
With this new data, the induction was confirmed.

Michael had a mind of his own. Apparently, he
wanted no part of the induction, either. At about
1:30 A.M. the Saturday before the scheduled induction, Michael was up to his usual tricks of producing
contractions, but this time they were significantly
different. Even so, I went back to bed. An hour
later, I was up with strong contractions that were
three to four minutes apart and lasting at least 90
seconds. I had passed the mucus plug and felt a lot
of pelvic pressure. I could feel him burrowing.

"Are you ready to come out?" I asked my belly.

At 4:30, I felt a small gush, followed by a larger
one, then a trickle. The flood gates had opened, and
at 5:00 I woke my husband. We called L&D triage,
and they told us to come in. I had Doug tidy the
house and do the dishes while I showered. If this
was the real McCoy, I was not returning to a messy
house, and from all the accounts I'd heard, it might
be the last long shower I would get for a while.

Having been warned by our birthing-class midwife that, once admitted, I would probably not be

allowed to eat solids, we got breakfast. Sitting on a puppy pad and wearing my Poise undergarments, I ate my breakfast in the car and talked to Michael. By 7:30, we were at the hospital.

The admitting nurse performed the routine and uncomfortable exams, confirmed labor, and admitted us. Thankfully, Michael picked an off-peak hour to start his performance, and we got the room that we desired—a large, private room with a hot tub for laboring. While we waited for the OB to finish an emergency delivery, we were cared for by Kristen, a certified nurse midwife. Kristen had us walk the halls, since I was still only 2 centimeters dilated. Doug and I walked together, talking to each other and to Bean, laughing, holding hands, and pausing every so often to squat during a contraction.

At about 11:00, the contractions became intermittently unbearable; Doug had to help me back up after each one. We returned to our room, and Kristen sought her superiors. We talked to Michael some more and told him that he was doing great. Now that it was a decent hour, Doug made the round of phone calls to inform family that we were at the hospital.

An attending physician finally arrived and examined me, only to find me 3 centimeters dilated and 100 percent effaced. "You have a bit more to go. Keep walking," I was told. Off she went. As she left, the anesthesiologists paid me a visit to ask about "pain management." Since I still had laryngitis, Doug translated my rasps. Handing them a copy of our birth plan, he explained that I wanted to go for as long as possible without medication, and if I changed my mind, an epidural was preferred.

More residents came in to prepare the postnatal equipment. One gave me an odd look as I swayed and alternated between squatting and kneeling instead of lying still in the bed.

Within the next hour, the waves of contractions intensified and were only 20 to 30 seconds apart. Kristen called the OB again to make sure that laboring in the hot tub was still plausible. The OB arrived, examined me, and as if I weren't there, announced, "The cervix is at five centimeters. Heartbeat's strong. It's okay for the tub."

With Kristen and Doug flanking me, I made the fifteen-foot journey to the hot tub, pausing every few minutes for another wave of intense, gripping contractions. Each one took me to my knees, and Kristen and Doug held my arms as I swooned. By the time we made it to the tub 30 minutes later, the contractions were so strong that getting in was impossible. No matter how badly I wanted the hydro-labor experience, it was not happening.

Caressing my belly, I told Michael, "I think we're going to meet each other soon."

Doug and Kristen assisted me back to the bed, and I got into a modified yoga child's pose. After watching two or three contractions that were literally off the charts, Kristen asked if I wanted the back upright so that I could hug it. It was pure genius. I got on my knees and hugged the back of the bed while the contractions continued, wave after wave. The contractions and I were one, and the experience transcended any sense of measurable time—that is until I had a contraction that was so deep it seemed nearly endless, the pressure on my cervix beyond what I could have ever imagined.

In a moment of personal weakness, I asked for the epidural. Kristen called the OB to check me internally again to make sure that I hadn't progressed too much for the epi. At 7 centimeters dilated, I was still within the acceptable limits. The anesthesiologists were paged, and we were told, "It could still be a while."

"Did you hear that?" I said to my belly.

The anesthesiologists prepared for their task, but before they got to have their fun, I had another contraction. I told Kristen that it felt like I had to push. She paged the OB, who'd been gone for only five minutes. The OB returned and wanted me to turn around.

I shook my head and told her in my raspy whisper, "Can't. Hurts. Too much. Feels. Like. I. Have-to. Poop."

"Are you sure?"

"Yes! Now!" I gasped as another intense contraction seized me.

I didn't know it then, but that very phrase—"Feels like I have to poop"—means that it's too late for an epidural. During this conversation, if you can call it that, the senior attending OB was paged.

She arrived, checked me, and announced in a thick German accent, "She's at nine-point-five. It's time."

In just a few short minutes, I had progressed an additional 2.5 centimeters.

Dr. German wanted to collapse the bed and get me on my back, and she was not taking no for an answer. Getting me there was pure hell. Anything was better than on my back. Someone set up the birthing bar as Doug and Kristen helped me turn around and assume the position, both trying to keep the covers on me. I didn't want covers. I had already ditched the hospital gown and my wedding bands, and I was close to taking out the intravenous prep that had been inserted in my right hand shortly after we were set up in the birthing room.

"No. No covers." I waved them off.

More contractions.

My husband interpreted my next set of raspy whisper-screams: "I. Have-to. Pushhhhhh. Now! I. Have-to. Poop!"

"Okay, dear . . . blah blah blah down," I heard from the disembodied German voice.

"Wha? . . . Okay."

"No, no, no, no! Schtop, schtop! I said, 'Scootch, scoootch.' Okay. A little tear on zee labia. But iz okay. Vee caught it in time."

"Oh. I heard—"

Another contraction.

"—push!"

Kristen and Doug coached me through the final waves of contractions as the pressure on my cervix intensified. They reminded me not to tense up and to ride through it. Doug chanted the affirmations we'd made during birthing class. I looked into his tear-filled eyes, and we exchanged "I love you's."

Dr. German encouraged me, too. "Okay. Von more. Big, push . . . Gut! Gut! Very nice."

Finally, at 2:43 P.M., Michael made his grand entrance.

He was placed on my belly. While Doug cut the umbilicus, I was prepared for delivering the placenta.

Michael entered the world vaginally without an epidural or episiotomy (despite my minor labial tear). As he lay on my belly, wet and wrinkled and fussing, I touched his head and whispered, "You did great." The pediatricians then whisked him away to the other side of the room to be examined, cleaned, diapered, and swaddled. He wailed, announcing his displeasure.

"That's good, Mama," one of the pediatricians said. "A good, healthy, robust cry."

Doug stayed by my side while I delivered the placenta and was cleaned up. As the pediatricians announced Michael's APGAR score, Doug zoomed the camera in on Michael and the pediatricians. One turned and said, "Dad, you can come over."

"I can? Really?"

"Sure thing. Come meet your son."

Doug looked at me. Elated but torn, he squeezed my hand and said, "I'll be right back."

"Go, go," I whispered.

"Hello, Beany, Beany, Beany," he said as he placed his hand on Michael's naked belly.

Michael stopped crying, turned his head, and looked right at his papa, as if to say, *Hey! I know that sound. Finally, something familiar.*

Had I not seen it occur on our birth video, I'd have thought, *Nah, that didn't happen.* But it did. Our newborn son found comfort in his father's voice, a voice he'd heard for forty weeks and six days.

After being cleaned, examined, and measured, Michael was returned to me for our first nursing. "I'm your mama. I've been waiting to meet you," I cooed, and kissed his forehead. Michael looked at me, looked at Doug, closed his eyes, and snuggled right in for a well-deserved nap after his delivery to his elderly prima gravida mama—knowing by our voices that he was in the loving care of his family.

Erika Swanson Geiss

Pig Doo and Foofy

A name is so important. You're stuck with it for your whole life, after all. As new parents, we rack our brains over all of the problems that come with choosing a name for someone else. What does it mean? Should it be a family name? Is it unique enough? Is it too common? Does the first name complement the last name? Is it easy to say? Does it rhyme with anything embarrassing? Would the initials be anything silly or a horrible acronym? My husband's are TLC, cute enough but better avoided.

My husband and I didn't make matters easier by choosing each other as partners. He's French; I'm American. The fact that the name had to work in two languages vastly reduced our possibilities; right away, it was clear that there would be no Madison and no Jean-Luc. Still, the lack of possibilities didn't make the decision any easier.

I wanted to name our daughter Natalie. I imagined a brunette beauty, bright-eyed and charming—like Natalie Wood or Natalie Portman. My husband said it was old-fashioned . . . in France. He wanted Chloe. I thought there were too many Chloe's in both countries.

Somewhere around the third choice for both of us was Justine. We both liked the name, which sounded chic and distinguished. Being named Justine, we thought, greatly increased one's chances of being an attorney rather than an exotic dancer. She would probably be dark-haired, like both of us, as well as serious, pretty, and smart.

Of course, when the actual baby joined us, it was difficult to reconcile the name Justine with her pink, bald, snorting reality. The first thing I said, in an epidural-driven fog, was, "You're such a little . . . piglet!" And she was, with her wonderful, rosy newborn color and mucus-filled nose.

In those early days in the hospital, the piglet metaphor stuck around longer than I expected. "The piglet is hungry." "The piglet is stinky." And finally, transforming itself into a term of endearment, "Who's Mommy's little piglet?" When we took her home, she was simply "Piglet" with a capital P.

Justine was forgotten. In fact, I don't think we used her real name at all in that first year, except when speaking of her to strangers who, otherwise, would have thought we were insane. At first, it was cute. Then, family members started to worry that she would attend kindergarten as "Piglet Callendrier" and be traumatized for life. We gave this only the mildest of considerations. We thought Piglet was sweet. If it was good enough for Pooh's sidekick, it was good enough for our child.

The problem came afterward with the mutation of the nickname. Piglet became Piggly Wiggly. Then Piggly Wiggly Woo. P-Woo. Piggy Doo. Piggy Doo Bear. We finally settled upon Pig Doo, and I couldn't tell you its origins if my life depended upon it. Justine was fond of Pig Doo, as well, and we happily sung her songs, replacing classic lyrics with Pig Doo: "And Pig Doo was her name-o . . ." "With a Pig Doo here, and a Pig Doo there . . ."

When my son was born, three years after Pig Doo, we spent far less time worrying about the name. We both liked the name David. It was my father-in-law's name, to boot. We paired it with my father's middle name, Arthur, and we had a winner, a name we both liked and a family-pleaser, too. Besides, we knew he wouldn't be David for long.

Around the time of David's birth, Justine had received some squirty bath toys as a gift. Mostly, they were starfish, with a turtle and fish thrown in for good measure. In an effort to combat her recent, impending-brother-induced bad behavior, I had given the starfish nicknames—"Whiny Starfish," "Bossy Starfish," "Noisy Starfish," and "Sweet Starfish." When we played, Bossy and Whiny were always a real pain, and Sweet saved the day every time. (With all this talk of starfish, you can see where this is going, can't you?)

The new baby was quickly the Hungry Starfish, the Sleepy Starfish, the Stinky Starfish, the Screaming Starfish, and finally, just Starfish. Starfish caught on like wildfire. The whole family referred to him as Starfish. He was a sturdy, muscular little baby; we thought he might be a boxer, perhaps—David "The Starfish" Callendrier. It was so popular that for six months there were zero mutations—no "star" or "fish" or any variation of either, until his nickname changed permanently.

Somewhere in the midst of the random baby babble that came out of our mouths when addressing our smallest one, we began to refer to our little starfish as "Foofy." If Starfish was catchy, Foofy was worse. Much like Pig Doo, we couldn't even really identify its origins, but there it was, and it was so darned cute, and he seemed like such a Foofy (whatever that is), that it stuck fast.

Early on, we worried about our kids being able to correctly identify their real names when it counted—outside the home, with teachers, for example. "Justine, *Justine!* **JUSTINE!** Could you answer the question, please?" Nevertheless, when Pig Doo and Foofy started day care, there was no mention of their silly nicknames, and they became Justine and David again. They understood that they have real names and home names and thought that everyone else should too.

In all their silliness, the nicknames mean that my children are loved, and it makes them feel special in a way that I never expected. When we moved houses, I painted a pig to hang on Justine's new wall and a starfish (not having any frame of reference for a foofy) for David. They love them unabashedly. I know that as adolescents, they'll kill us if we so much as breathe a word of Pig Doo and Foofy to their friends, but for now, Foofy likes being Foofy as much as Pig Doo likes being Pig Doo. Their little friends are actually envious and wonder why they don't have a "home" name too.

And the answer to that? The world is filled with Davids and Justines; they will meet many of them throughout their lives and no doubt even befriend a few. But no one, and I mean no one, is named Pig Doo or Foofy. That's got to make a kid feel good.

Amanda Callendrier

Feeding Jackson

"Leeann?" she called.

She'd seen me first, before I had a chance to wedge my body between her and my grocery cart.

"Let me take a look at that beautiful baby!" Gina was always enthusiastic. Sometimes too enthusiastic. But this time she was right. Jackson was beautiful. A perfect, soft, chubby body wrapped in blue fleece, sleeping obliviously in his brand-new car seat in the bottom of the plastic Wal-Mart cart.

But when Gina leaned in for a better view and a whiff of that fresh baby smell, she saw my illicit goods. "Leeann?" she asked, unable to believe her eyes. "What are you doing? Are you sure you want to do this?"

That's what I'd asked myself as I'd buckled Jackson into his car seat. And again as I drove to the store. And kept asking as I'd pushed the oversized cart to the back corner where they stocked the baby formula. I'd continued to question myself as I scanned the shelves, read the labels, and selected three of the heavy tin cans. I'd placed them beside the car seat, next to the "closest thing to mom" rubber nipples and plastic baby bottles. Then I'd hunched over my cart, red-faced, hoping to get to the checkout counter and out the door before I was spotted by anyone I knew. That is never easy in a small town. Especially not when you're buying something you'd rather not be seen with.

Gina had realized the shocking truth. I was going to bottle-feed my baby.

"But you were going to breastfeed!" she gasped. "And it's so much better not to supplement with formula. Why are you buying these things?"

I started to cry. Gut-wrenching, shoulder-shaking sobs. It woke Jackson and he joined in. My breasts leaked, drenching the pads in my nursing bra and soaking through the maternity T-shirt that hung over the loose flesh of my stomach.

"I really need to get home," I said, looking down at the floor and pushing the cart past Gina.

"You can't really want to do this," Gina called after me as I headed toward the long lines snaking in front of the checkout counters. "I know women get a bit sore at first. But you only get one chance at this, you know. It's not too late to reconsider."

"Reconsider." As if it had been a spur-of-the-moment decision. As if I'd been driving by Wal-Mart and suddenly thought to myself, "Hmm, maybe it would be a good idea to buck nature and thousands of experts and buy a can of beige powder to feed my baby." I'd reconsidered, all right. Considered and reconsidered and reconsidered again.

Of course, I'd planned to breastfeed. I'd heard about the benefits. All the women I knew had either breastfed their babies or planned to in the future. Although the media still covers controversies about women breastfeeding in "inappropriate" public places, my female friends would have been more outraged to see a woman bottle-feeding in public. Doctors, nurses, friends, websites, magazines, and parenting books all said that breastfeeding was the natural and best way, and I'd assumed it would be the choice for me. Until it wasn't.

In the middle of the night on Jackson's one-week birthday, I was holding him in the new rocking chair in our living room. He was hungry. I was exhausted. We were both frustrated. I stared at my watch, counting down the seconds. Three . . . two . . . one. Finally. Ten minutes were up, and I could pry Jackson off my stinging right nipple and move

him to my left breast. Relief was short-lived. Jackson
was barely latched on to my left nipple when the new
pain started. My nipples were tender bleeding scabs.
Jackson eyed me suspiciously and frowned. Two days
earlier, I'd dispatched my husband to the drugstore
for the nipple creams Gina had recommended. So
far, they hadn't helped me, and Jackson clearly didn't
like the flavor.

Jackson was a typical healthy newborn, crying
for food every four hours. This was perfectly normal
for him, but not nearly enough rest between feedings
for my aching nipples. Or for my mind.

On the eighth night Jackson woke at 3:00 A.M.
I carried him to the living room, and once again
we sat in the rocking chair, with Jackson sucking
greedily, working my breast to get enough food for
his empty tummy, while I concentrated on my digital
watch. The lack of sleep, the surging hormones, and
the pain were suddenly all too much and I started
to cry. What was wrong with me? Didn't I love my
wonderful baby enough to tolerate a little pain? I
sobbed and sobbed. Salty tears fell down onto Jackson's working cheek.

My husband stumbled into the living room in his
underwear to see what was going on. "This has to
stop," he said. "This isn't good for you. And Jackson
needs a happy mom."

He was right.

The books said breastfeeding would help me forge a stronger bond with my new baby. For me, breastfeeding had built a brick wall between me and this tiny creature. But could I stop? Were the experts right? Would bottle-feeding damage my perfect baby? And what would my friends say? Would they shun me? Lecture me? Maybe women I didn't know would see me bottle-feeding in public and harangue me. If Jackson were bottle-fed and developed asthma later, it would be my fault. Would bottle-feeding lower his IQ? I kept fretting and crying, while my husband put his arm around me and Jackson slurped on my scabbed nipple.

The next morning I searched the Internet for support. But all the sites I found sung the praises of breastmilk, damning formula-feeders as lazy and uncaring. One site assumed that irresponsible bottle-feeding mothers wouldn't cuddle or bond with our children, that we would just lay our babies on the floor at feeding time, propping up their bottles with blankets and pillows, presumably so we could use both hands to drink gin and run the television remote during feeding time. Obviously, I was the worst mother in the world. I had been so lucky to get this perfect baby, and I couldn't even feed him properly.

But I simply could not breastfeed this baby.

And how would I tell my friends? Jen might understand; she had no children. But Anna was a member of La Leche League; there was no way she'd speak to me once she found out about this. And Gina had sent me a half dozen books on the benefits of breastfeeding the day she'd found out I was pregnant.

By the time I got home from Wal-Mart with my bottle-feeding supplies, my breasts were hard as rocks and leaking though my jacket. The motion of the moving car had lulled Jackson to sleep, but the trip from car to house woke him and his hungry crying started again.

In the kitchen, I lifted the can of formula to read the directions on the side. A bright warning added to the label announced, "Breastmilk is the best way to feed your baby." I cut the side of my hand on the sharp can while opening the lid, and my dark red blood dripped down onto the countertop. It seemed to take hours to measure the sticky powder. I stirred it with a spoon, but the fine dust turned to a lumpy mess until I finally dug the hand blender out of the back of the cupboard. When I'd finally mixed it smooth, I heated the foul-smelling concoction in the microwave and then tested it on my wrist, just like they did in the movies. At last, I was finally ready to feed my crying, red-faced baby.

I carried Jackson and the warm bottle back to the rocking chair. He lifted his head expectantly, and I held the rubber nipple up to his open lips. He bent forward to pull the smooth tip into his mouth and sucked. Formula flowed into his little mouth, much faster than he'd been able to access milk from my scratchy nipples. Jackson's body relaxed, suddenly relieved, as if he had been roaming the desert for weeks without water and had suddenly come across a fountain. His eyes bulged with gratitude and looked up at me accusingly, as if to ask why I'd been holding out on him all this time. I leaned forward to kiss his tiny forehead, and his miniature hand reached up and landed on my cheek. He let out a sigh. Content.

Today, Jackson is an energetic eighteen-month-old toddler. He's unreasonably healthy, rarely even gets colds. He spills over with life and happiness— grinning, laughing, learning to talk, playing simple teasing games, and running around the house, backward, sideways, and with his blanket over his head. Even Gina admits that he's turned out well.

Sure, breastfeeding has many benefits. But I loved Jackson the best way I could, squeezing as much enjoyment as possible out of every cuddle while he drank from his bottle.

When I look back now, deciding to bottle-feed Jackson seems inconsequential, just one of the hundreds of agonizing decisions I've already made about his care. Do I vaccinate him and risk autism? Do I quit my job to stay home with him and risk him having no social skills? Gina was right about making choices; you usually get only one chance. And every choice has a lifelong impact. Eventually, these choices will add up to become my son's life and my legacy. Onlookers judge every action. Some decisions will be right, and some will be wrong. All I can do is love Jackson and make the best decisions I can.

Leeann Minogue

Under a Starlit Sky

At the doctor's office I thumbed through baby magazines, but my headache made it difficult to focus. I quit reading and glanced at the clock. What if my husband didn't make it in time for the ultrasound?

Terry rushed in just as the nurse's aide called out my name. "Sorry I'm late," he said.

I squeezed his hand as he helped me up. "I'm just glad you're here. I wouldn't want you to miss this."

Inside the little white room the aide took my vitals, then frowned. "Your blood pressure is high."

"Is everything okay?" I asked, as she walked toward the door. I looked at my husband, worried.

She turned around. "I need to get the doctor, but you're going to be just fine, dear."

But somehow I wasn't so sure. I'd seen the look on her face.

The doctor confirmed my worst fears. "You have toxemia. The symptoms include headache, swelling, elevated blood pressure, and protein in the urine. These disappear after delivery, which we must try to postpone to make the fetus more viable. You must be hospitalized immediately; no going home. I need to warn you, this is a very serious matter. You could both die."

"Die?" I said in disbelief. None of the classes I'd taken, nothing I had read or done these past few months had prepared me for this. All I could think of was the suitcase at home, packed and ready for the momentous occasion when my water would break at some ungodly hour and my husband would rush me to the hospital in our little Toyota. Now, everything had changed. We could die.

Just as there was no time to go home and get that suitcase, there was no time to suppress the delivery. Worried about dying, my blood pressure had sky-rocketed. When admitted, I was already dilated two centimeters.

Chris, our firstborn, was delivered only a few hours later—a handsome red-haired boy weighing three and a half pounds. He was so small his father could hold him in the palms of his hands. Chris had to remain in intensive care for five weeks, with the miracle of modern technology simulating my womb.

Wires, tubes, and monitors surrounded him constantly. So did an excellent nursing staff. He soon became one of their favorites. "He's a real fighter," they'd tell me every day. "His red hair suits him."

For the first week I couldn't hold him. And it was weeks before I could nurse. But the kind staff showed me how to express my milk so I wouldn't lose it. Soon I became a dairy farm. The staff bottled my extra milk and used it for the other preemies in the ward whose mothers were unable to nurse. Like Rosasharn in Steinbeck's *The Grapes of Wrath*, I was providing milk. But this milk was not for a feeble elderly person; but rather, for fragile, untimely born infants.

Each day the favorite part of my visit was when I could sit by Chris as he lay outside the incubator under specialized heat lamps that kept his body temperature constant. Wrapping my hand around his little fingers, tinier than a doll's, I'd talk and sing to him for hours. Often I'd close my eyes and just pray and try to keep from nodding off.

As the weeks passed, the daily visits began to take their toll on me. Even though my blood pressure had returned to normal, my headaches continued.

I was sent to a specialist. "They'll get better once your baby comes home," he said. He returned my chart to the plastic box on his door, clicked his pen a couple of times, and stared at me gravely as he said, "But if I were you, I wouldn't get pregnant again. Evolution has not designed you to have babies. Next time could prove fatal for you and the fetus."

Stunned and dismayed, I left his office. What right had he to say that to me? He wasn't even an obstetrician.

A few days later, a friend living near the hospital offered me her home to rest in during my daily visits. This helped tremendously, and soon my headaches disappeared. Three weeks later, Chris was able to come home weighing a healthy five pounds.

After this traumatic beginning, I wanted to make life as normal as possible for the three of us. Months later, I asked myself, "What could be more normal than camping?" My husband and I had always loved the outdoors, and we needed some fun.

With our pediatrician's approval, we took Chris on his first camping trip, just prior to his first birthday. Before baby, Terry and I had taken frequent trips to Yosemite National Park. Although we knew we wouldn't be able to take him hiking up Half-Dome, there were plenty of other day hikes we could enjoy together.

California poppies in full bloom competed with our son's orange-red hair as we made our way along the freeway. A few hours later, we drove into Yosemite

Valley—the place that had brought us so many happy memories. We got out of the car and filled our lungs with fresh mountain air. Half-Dome loomed above us in all her glory, just as she always had every year before.

The first few days were great. Chris loved Bridal Veil Falls and the hike near El Capitan. But after a few nights, he had a hard time falling asleep in the tent. He'd developed an ear infection. We hadn't planned on that. We had to drive out of the valley to a doctor's office in order to get a prescription. Until the medicine took effect, we all suffered. Night after night, Terry and I took turns rocking Chris to sleep in our arms, far, far away from the rest of the campers in order to not disturb them. This was particularly hard, given the fact that the Yosemite Valley tends to greatly amplify all sound. But somehow we managed.

One evening, as I was wishing I'd had the foresight to squeeze into the car a rocking chair, automatic swing, and a host of antibiotics, I was haunted by the headache specialist's words, "You're not cut out to be a mom." This mantra filled my head as Chris continued to cry miserably. I tried desperately to comfort him, even though I longed to fall asleep.

What had I been thinking, anyway? I thought, sinking deeper into self-pity. *No one else has a crying baby here. Just me.*

My mind continued to drift further into negative self-talk, and before I knew it, I'd walked deeper into the woods. *Where am I?* I worried. *What if I can't find my way back to the tent?*

Quickly, I looked around and discovered familiar markings. The day before we'd passed this way returning from a hike. Terry had noticed a few logs that had been cut down and placed in a circle. We'd thought this would be a great place to roast marshmallows some night when we weren't so sleep deprived.

Rocking Chris in my arms, I moved toward the center of the circle. I tried to ignore my back, which ached from carrying him for so long, and focused on the fact that at least he was almost asleep. I let out a sigh of relief and took a moment to drink in the scent of deep forest pine. I wanted to just *be* for a moment. It had been so long. I could almost hear the beating of my heart; the forest was so still.

And then I looked up.

Pine trees stood tall and strong. They reached up toward the night sky and framed a countless host of stars that sparkled upon a midnight canvas. Their beauty captivated me, and I wanted to savor this moment—hold it in my hand like stardust and never let it go.

At home the city lights veiled the stars, and when camping before, I'd always been asleep by now. I would never have seen such a starlit sky had it not been for my little boy. It was his troubles that had brought me here to this place. And with that realization, I also realized that ever since he'd been born, my son had been taking me on one unplanned, unexpected journey after another.

Babies do such things. They are a lot of work and require endless amounts of sacrifice, which can be tough when the mother is self-centered and inexperienced, as I was then. Yet, somehow, in taking care of our babies, we learn from them how to give and how to grow beyond ourselves to become something more, something better.

That night, looking up at the stars so vast and far away, my problems seemed small and insignificant in comparison to their splendor. In my delirious, sleep-deprived state, they seemed to cry out to me, *Hey, remember that headache specialist? Well, he got it wrong.* You can never be one hundred percent prepared for motherhood, because it is motherhood itself that prepares you.

Deanna Stollar

Bonded for Life

I stood in the shower crying as milk poured from my swollen breasts like two faucets I couldn't turn off.

"Nobody told me about this," I sobbed to my husband, a complaint that had become my mantra over those first few weeks of motherhood. I'm sure he didn't know what he was getting into either. As he stared back at me, I saw a reflection of how crazy I had become. I was a woman possessed. My body was not my own anymore, and I would have to learn to accept it.

I had been so anxious for the baby to come and so tired of being pregnant. My mother told me to enjoy my time now because "once that baby comes, your life will never be the same." I didn't listen. I wished the time away, checking the toilet paper every hour for the slightest evidence of a loose mucus plug. I fantasized about where I would be when my water broke, maybe the grocery store, water gushing onto aisle nine. Then someone would call for "clean up" over the P.A. system, and I would be rushed home to have the baby.

But that wasn't how it happened. I resorted to all of the tricks—walking, castor oil, having sex. But nothing worked. Finally, after nine hours of active labor, in his own sweet time, Alex was born.

From the moment his broad shoulders abruptly pushed their way into my life, my firstborn filled my world with surprises. Our Bradley instructor had said that once you push the baby's head out, it's over. She never mentioned the shoulders. "Nobody told me about this part," I screamed as they came through the birth canal. That was the only sound I made the entire labor, and it was the moment I knew that if I had been at the hospital, I would have taken the drugs. But I was birthing the baby at home, and pain medication wasn't an option.

I also didn't know how completely I would fall in love with this child, how everything he did from birth on would impress me. I thought he was the most amazing baby that had ever been born. "He's advanced for his age," his father and I would agree behind closed doors. We made note of his extraordinary talents when we compared him to the other children in our birthing group.

"Wow, he's already sitting up," everyone said at our first get-together after the babies were born.

We were so proud, sure that our parenting skills had something to do with it. In reality, Alex was born several weeks before the other children, but that didn't stop us from gloating. We never considered that all of the other parents were secretly comparing their children to ours, certain that their new bundle of joy was the most amazing baby ever born.

We also witnessed some amazing parenting styles at that first postbirth reunion. "When he doesn't want to go to sleep, we just hold him down until he stops crying; it really works," said the dad of the largest boy there. His wife nodded in hesitant agreement, while my husband and I listened with wide-eyed disbelief. We were drawn to a more gentle approach to parenting. After reading a book called *The Continuum Concept* during my pregnancy, we were convinced that creating a strong bond of attachment when a child is young would lead to a confident, independent adulthood. We still believe that to be true, but at the time we didn't realize the side effects.

In the beginning, when we were still reading parenting books, I worried about not bonding enough.

I had heard horror stories about mothers who failed to bond with their babies. However, for us, bonding too little was never the problem. I instantly attached myself to Alex as if with Krazy Glue, the adhesive advertised as "strong enough to hold a man suspended in mid-air." When we were considering the benefits of attachment parenting, nobody told us about the possibility of becoming too attached. We didn't picture the construction worker from the Krazy Glue commercial, attached to a steel beam by his hard hat. We just felt warm and cuddly, imagining all the closeness we would experience as our child grew.

And we definitely were close. We made the decision to bring Alex into our bed partly for convenience and partly to prevent him from feeling separation anxiety. It seemed unnatural to put an infant in a room down the hall alone while we slept securely in each other's arms.

But the physical closeness had personal drawbacks for me. Sometimes I wondered if I would ever get my body back. Nursing on demand felt like a full-time job, especially when Kai, our second son, came along nineteen months later and I was still nursing Alex.

Then, they were both in our bed. We thought if we waited until Kai was ready to move into his own room, it would be a smoother transition for Alex. The upside was that Alex wasn't jealous of the new baby. He accepted his role as big brother beautifully and has always taken that role very seriously. When Kai didn't get his way with me, he often went to Alex for comfort, almost as a third parent. As they grew older, Kai depended on Alex for a bedtime story when I was busy with Keenan, who was born two and a half years after Kai.

Somehow, I thought the family-bed concept would play out differently. I saw the value of sleeping with our sons during their infancy, but I didn't realize how hard it would be to eventually get them into their own bed. As a new mother, I imagined one year of snuggling, and then I thought that Alex, on his first birthday, would politely ask his father and me for his own room, like a teenager asking to borrow the car keys. We would watch him toddle down the hall with his blanky to his own bed in his own room. The next morning, when we awoke from a full night's sleep, he would be in the kitchen flipping pancakes and making the coffee. But that's not how it went. Five years and three kids later, our bedroom was wall-to-wall bed. I remember climbing over four bodies just to get up to go to the bathroom at night.

Needless to say, with three children in our bed, romance took a back seat to our parenting duties, but it didn't disappear. We became more creative and learned to expand the definition of "date" to include a trip to the grocery store or sneaking ice cream out of the freezer while the kids were in the other room. Some of the decisions we made in the name of responsible parenting even enhanced our relationship, like getting rid of our television for a few years. We started reading to each other instead. The erotic literature of Anaïs Nin replaced mind-numbing episodes of *Friends*.

Now, the family bed is a distant memory. Alex, six feet tall with those same broad shoulders, turned eighteen this year. I am happy to report that he has been sleeping in his own bed for thirteen of those years. He is confident and independent, a talented athlete, musician, and scholar. But what I am most proud of is that he is comfortable in his own skin. He recently informed me that I am going to have to start loosening my grip and that his eventually moving out on his own had been the point all along. He says it would be good to start practicing that now, since he will be heading off to college in a matter of months.

Nobody told me how hard it would be to let him go. It's strange to think how out of touch with reality I was as a new mother. I couldn't have imagined the magnitude of the bond we would form. At first, it was Alex who seemed to need the bond the most, but then, somewhere along the way, everything changed. Now, here I am, hanging by my hat from that steel beam, feet dangling, wondering how the heck I am going to get down. And we are all thinking that maybe it would have been better to use something less permanent, like Elmer's glue or double-sided tape.

LeeAnn Elder Dakers

The Sisterhood of Motherhood

Once the baby is born, the first things that seem to go (besides your freedom and life as you used to know it) are the maternity clothes. Who among us isn't glad to give away the stretch-panel pants, the extra-full baby-doll blouses, and the sack-like pinafores to the first unsuspecting pregnant woman who crosses our path? Our battle cries echo down the halls of the maternity wards: "When do I get my body back?"

We save baby's first blanket or the tiny sweater hand-knitted by Aunt Penny, but few of us fondly keep the generously cut maternity capris that got us through that long, hot summer. Maternity clothes are best kept in active circulation.

Yet, when I search through my photograph albums from those pregnancy years, now twenty years ago (yikes!), there's one picture that makes me laugh and reflect on the sisterhood of motherhood. It involves a certain maternity T-shirt dress.

In the photo, I am posing arabesque at nine months pregnant, an unlikely ballerina in a rosy pink cotton jersey knit dress, looking about as graceful as an elephant en pointe. My sister took the photo of me goofing off in front of the camera to pass the last days of a very overdue delivery.

The dress was given to me by a friend who had recently had a baby. With the intensity of a car saleswoman, Erin had extolled the virtues of this dress that seemed to know no stretch limit. "It's the most comfortable thing you'll ever wear," she said. "No rubbing or chafing. Take it, please take it!"

I was grateful for any help I could get. After all, who wants to spend a lot of money on clothes that aren't going to rate a hanger in the closet as soon as you place the *pièce de résistance* in the bassinet? Let's face it, if you've chosen to nurse, as soon as the baby comes, it's all about buttoning down or pulling up the shirt about every other minute of the day. So I took the giant pink tunic that it was, and just as Erin had predicted, it became my second skin.

My sister flew all the way from New York City to Oregon, where I live, to be with me for the birth of my second child. She was herself two months pregnant. She really wanted to witness a birth firsthand before she had her baby. She also came to lend some much-needed support in the first week or two after the baby was born.

This was my second birth, so when the labor began I was as prepared as anyone can be. And I had the pink T-shirt dress on at the birthing center until the very last contraction. Yes, it was hiked up pretty far those last few hours. I remember my sister giving me a massage somewhere during the agony and the ecstasy of labor. I can still feel her hands digging into my straining back muscles, right through the fabric of that dress. Since this was natural childbirth, that massage was the closest thing I had to an epidural. At the time it seemed crazy, but I thought, *Sis, you give a really mean back rub. Who knew? I definitely owe you one!*

After Benjamin was born and the nursing began, the dress ended up in a heap on the floor. Just like when we were girls, my sister eyed my (pregnancy) clothes. I didn't even ask to borrow one of her shirts as collateral; I gladly passed along the pink T-shirt dress and all the stretch pants she could cram into her suitcase. She was happy she'd seen her first birth, gotten to rock her new nephew, and snagged some maternity clothes. I was happy to have had her help during that first intense week and to share that inde-scribable birth time with her. It was hard to say goodbye to my sister, and sending the dress along with her was like sending a piece of my heart along too.

Over the next seven months we kept in touch as much as we could. It's difficult when you are a new mother to even make a phone call, much less have a coherent conversation beyond what's the best diaper for the money. She naturally complained about weight gain, stretch marks, and swollen feet, but the one thing she loved was how accommodating the pink T-shirt dress was.

Late one February evening I received a call, or should I say *the* call.

"It hurts, it hurts, it hurts! Help me! No amount of book reading or Lamaze classes really prepared me for this. What do I do?"

"You just breathe. The pain is good. It means your baby is about to be born." I took on the tone of a firm, but loving, midwife. In fact, I think it was the exact same thing my midwife had said to me when I was in the same boat.

"Where are you?" I added.

"At home. They said it's still too early to come in to the midwife center."

"In that case, you ain't seen nothin' yet," I joked. "Have you got everything packed?"

"Of course, everything is packed! That happened weeks ago. By the way, I'm wearing that pink T-shirt dress you gave me. I've lived in it these past few months . . . *Pant, pant, hee, hee, whuh, whuh.*"

"Oh, cool, can I borrow that black sweater of yours now?"

"Ha, ha! Stop making me laugh. It makes my stomach hurt . . . *Hee, hee, huuhh!*"

Her contractions grew more intense, and we stayed on the phone together for more than an hour, until it was time for her to go to the birthing center. Somehow, that pink T-shirt dress brought my sister and me together by its very threads. I wished I could have been all the way across the country during the delivery, but I like to think my love and energy was embedded somewhere between the warp and the woof of that dress, giving her some comfort when she needed it.

After my niece was born, my mother went to help my sister those first few weeks. I got to talk to my sister on the phone for a brief minute or two, in between the feedings, diaperings, and naps.

"Thanks for the help during the birth, Sis," she said. "I told my friends about our phone call, and they said we should use it to pitch to AT&T as a long-distance phone commercial."

"Happy to be able to help."

"By the way," she added, "guess who phoned me the other day."

"Who?"

"Your old friend Jennifer, from high school."

"Yeah, I gave her your number months ago. Glad she finally gave you a call. I'm sure she told you she's pregnant now too. It's an epidemic!"

"She did," said my sister. "In fact, she's coming over next week to visit me and the baby. I've got a big pile of maternity clothes to give her. Of course, the only thing she'll really like is that pink T-shirt dress . . ."

Elizabeth King Gerlach

Mothering from Scratch

My son was three and a half when I became a new mom for the second time. What I learned in those first few hours as the mother of two was more than what was offered in any best-selling book of maternal expectations. It didn't take long to realize that I was an expert only at being my little boy's mom and that, when it came to my newborn daughter, I was mothering from scratch.

At the time of Chloe's birth, I considered myself a veteran of the mommy wars. I'd already chosen a preschool and mastered the carpool line. But when they rolled that clear bassinet containing my newborn, swaddled in a hospital-issue blanket and cap, into my hospital room, I quickly discovered I was back to being a private. That's when a portly nurse who had recently had a good night's sleep pulled rank and blindsided me.

"She's supposed to be in the newborn nursery so I can sleep," I told the nurse candidly. I was exhausted, which was a good cover for being pissed off. There was no pretense after a second cesarean and a morphine drip. I knew that sleep would be at even more of a premium once we got home. "Take her back," I insisted.

"She's keeping the other babies awake," the nurse said.

How could my daughter, at a mere four hours old, be causing a commotion? Through my morphine-induced fog, I contemplated my options and realized I had none. I then hallucinated being called into the principal's office in the not-too-distant future with my daughter at the center of some havoc. Then my thoughts flashed back to the serene life formerly known as mine. Zachary, my son, was never at the nexus of an uproar, not even during his "terrible" twos. My head began to spin as it occurred to me that juggling car seats would be the easiest of my upcoming tricks. Having already had one baby under my belt didn't give me a lick of insight into what this new child would be like or what I'd need to do to be a good mother to her.

What everyone had told me was true: no two children are the same. What they hadn't told me is that, despite your best intents and purposes, you can't be the same mother to each child. Before my daughter's birth, I'd really thought that, aside from buying pink bedding and learning to push a double-stroller down the big box–store aisles, I'd be doing everything basically the same way I'd done it with my son. I thought her needs would be the same, at least as a baby. Eat, poop, sleep. Eat, poop, sleep. I thought she would be a baby who, like my son, would swing in the baby swing while I sang songs and polished my nails. I thought she would let me watch soaps while her brother was at school and she slept for so long that I would check the bassinet in the bedroom to make sure she was breathing. I was wrong. Her relentless crying was always a clear indication that Chloe was breathing. And she rarely, if ever, slept in the bassinet like Zachary had.

So I learned to catnap on the sofa while Chloe slept in the swing. I learned how to fit a chair next to the dryer so she could sit atop it in her car seat, where she'd bounce around and somehow be soothed into her longest nap of twenty minutes. And I learned how to drive the preschool carpool with a sleeping infant. As Chloe got older, I grew accustomed to shuffling her from hip to hip while I played with her brother or did household chores. She slept only when I garnered no personal benefit or break at all.

Chloe responded differently than her brother had to stories, songs, formula, food, and car rides. He fell asleep to music with the light on; she needed the room to be quiet and dark. She talked sooner and walked later than her brother. Once Chloe could roll, she would roll around on a blanket—back and forth, forth and back—for a solid hour each night, making me dizzy but also making me laugh—while her brother quietly rolled Hot Wheels along the arm of the sofa. And before long, I just rolled with their differences as well.

Then one day during that first winter, I found my groove. I was standing and swaying with six-month-old Chloe on my left hip the way she liked. Balancing Zachary's oversized book of nursery rhymes on the top of the dresser, I was turning the pages with my right hand as we went through the book eleven times just the way he liked. With rhythms that seemed as different as when I'd tried in vain to pat my stomach and rub my head, I was parenting my two children separately but in sync. And no one was more surprised at how natural it all felt than I was.

Sometime between Chloe's cruising phase and walking phase, I learned a lesson from my baby daughter that transcended the boundaries of motherhood. By rocking the baby boat, she had taught me to go with the flow. I figured out new ways of doing old things and how to go in two directions at once, scaling the stumbling blocks of duplex-parenting in a single bound. I realized that was exactly what I could expect as the mother of two—and that it was my kids' right to expect that from me.

Amy Nathan

This story was first published on the WashingtonPost.com blog, November 27, 2007.

Knit One, Hurl Two

Some new mothers are naturals. They brag about how "easy" the birthing process was, the sleepless weeks never show on their faces, and they display an amazing amount of expertise with all the latest equipment and products for those new babies. Then there are the mothers like me. I had absolutely no experience with babies prior to the birth of my son, and I mean no experience whatsoever. I've been told that I had a Betsy Wetsy doll when I was about five, but what the nurse brought me for that first feeding was no pink plastic doll.

Shortly after my son's birth, the head nurse had told me that he was unnerving the staff. Whereas most newborns sleep quite a bit after their trying ordeal, mine was wide awake and watching the nurses as they went about their duties. When they brought him to me for his first feeding, he was staring at me with that same intense look, as if to say, *Who made you my mother?* From our first encounter, my son knew that I did not have a shred of an idea as to what I was doing.

Breastfeeding was a novel experience, to say the least. I had gone through the training, and I had asked the right questions. I thought I knew what to expect. When my son latched on with a gusto that convinced me I had stuck my breast into an industrial-strength vacuum, it was obvious that he was the one in charge, not I. He tried to keep that serious look on his face during these sessions, but I have to admit that he looked a bit silly with that milk-induced look of euphoria on his face. It is a good thing that I was a successful nurser, because when I tried to put together one of those just-like-mom–type bottles, the nipple went flying one way while the contents splashed against the opposite wall. My son was not amused.

Diapers were another adventure. Most of my friends, trying to be helpful, had bought newborn-sized diapers for my son. They didn't take the hint that, before his birth, my mother referred to him as "Moose," and that when he was born, they had to turn his foot sideways on the birth certificate because his footprint wouldn't fit into the pro-vided space on the form. So newborn diapers were definitely out, along with the hundreds of dollars' worth of newborn clothing that my family and friends had given me. It's just as well that my son didn't have any high-fashion ideas, because he spent the first year of his life in onesies.

Right about the time I started to feel a little bit confident about my role as a new mother, another crisis arose. I would like to know why no one warned me about how tricky boys can be on the changing table. Once, when I dropped the powder, I didn't know to cover his front with the diaper while I reached down to the floor for my item. As if on cue, it started raining in my house. Drenched with baby pee, I stood up and saw what I could've sworn was a baby-sized smirk on my infant's face. My credibility with him had yet to be firmly established.

I tried to be the best mother that I could be. I was able to stay home that first year, so I watched every show on babies that I could find. After the show that advised me to feed my son only fresh, natural foods, I went out and purchased a food mill. My son looked skeptically at the contents of his bowl and wouldn't eat until I popped open a jar of some salt- and sugar-laden baby food. As a side note, I knew early on that my son had artistic ability. After a meal of strained peas, sweet potatoes, and green beans, I opened his diaper to find my son's attempt at Monet's *Water Lilies*. Quite nice.

That first year, I watched shows about exercise, how to teach children to read, and child safety. I learned how to do baby CPR in case of an emergency, though I couldn't imagine holding my son on one arm, his head toward the floor, pounding on his back. After the show, he cocked one eyebrow at me as if to say, *Don't even think about it.* I assured him that I would never dream of damaging his dignity in such a manner. We went along like this for several weeks, until my son's curiosity brought on The Incident.

I had taken up knitting, and not being the organized person that I wish I was, I usually left various pieces of knitting paraphernalia around the apartment. I was trying to knit a yellow-ducky sweater vest for my son when I noticed that he had a strange expression on his face . . . on his blue face. My son was unable to breathe. Without thinking, I grabbed him, draped him over one arm, and pounded him sharply on the back. *Kerpop!* Out came a stitch marker, a tiny round piece of plastic that was made to fit over a knitting needle. Along with the marker came oatmeal, some milk, and various-colored contents of baby food jars. There would be no impressionist artwork on the changing table that night.

When I rolled my son back over, the look on his face was one of wonder and amazement. He looked me right in the eye, his bug-eyed blue, mine teary brown, and if he could've shaken hands with me at that moment, he would've done it. Every expectation, every disappointment, every doubt about what I was doing evaporated. I dropped to the floor and hugged my son with every bit of love and joy and relief in my body. When I sat back with him on my lap, he was smiling. My son liked me. He really liked me. Sally Field at the Oscars had nothing on me.

From that time on, things were different between my son and me. My approval rating did slip a bit when, a week later, my husband and I ran out of the apartment during an earthquake, leaving our son in his crib. But a trip to a local restaurant that had various flavors of gelatin blocks on the salad bar did much to repair that tiny breach. My son's diapers were especially interesting that evening.

Patricia L. Crawford

Mom Overboard!

This was my first outing as a mother of two, and I'd prepared for it like a climber about to scale Mount Everest. The diaper bag was loaded with colic medicine, breast pads, wipes, diapers in two sizes, little containers of Cheerios, anything and everything I thought I might need for an hour away with a newborn and a twenty-month-old. I tried to think of everything, cover all my bases. I was ready. At least I hoped I was. I strapped both girls in their car seats, took a deep breath, and got behind the wheel for the first time in three weeks, thinking, *I can do this.*

The first few minutes went well. Molly slept in her carrier nestled in the shopping cart. That didn't leave much room for groceries, but it couldn't be helped. As I lifted Haley up into the cart, I smelled a familiar odor. "Poo Poo," she crooned proudly. No kidding. "There's a changing table in the ladies' room at the far end of the store," a clerk informed me. I headed that way.

As we walked, shopper after shopper stopped to admire Baby Molly, completely ignoring Haley. Haley squirmed and twisted around in the seat, trying to get their attention. When this didn't work, she grabbed a roll of paper towels off the shelf and dropped it on Molly's head. Molly wailed, and in my sleep-deprived state, I started crying too. We were barely inside the front door. I hadn't placed a single thing in the cart. This was not looking good.

I scrambled to unstrap Molly from her carrier. Then Haley started crying too. The second I picked up Molly, my breasts took it as their cue and started gushing. The breast pads packed neatly in the diaper bag did me no good; the front of my blouse was soaked in seconds.

Seeing me hold Molly, Haley started screaming, "I wanna get down! I wanna get down!"

I felt like everyone was looking at me and thought of making a dash for the parking lot. Maybe we can eat next week.

With my free hand, I lifted Haley out of the cart. As soon as her feet hit the floor, she took off running down the aisle and out of sight. What a spectacle I must have been scrambling after her, a squalling baby in my arms, tears streaming down my face, my blouse soaked with breastmilk.

I was wrong, I thought. *I can't do this.* All I wanted to do was take my two babies home, crawl under the covers, and never venture out again.

I caught up with Haley two aisles away and sat down on the floor beside her, exhausted and dejected. I felt like I hadn't slept in months. Other shoppers passed. A mom with older kids half-smiled. Another looked at me, then turned and walked the other way. I thought, *Surely, they remember what this is like.* Then I thought of my sisters, who have four and five kids each. They make it look so easy. I bet they never fell to pieces on the floor of the dog food aisle.

I mustered what strength I had and got back to my feet. From somewhere in my cobwebby mind came an old trick of my mom's. I started singing, "We're almost finished. Then we're going home. Haley is a good girl." Haley stopped crying, more surprised than consoled. I coaxed her back to the cart, propped Molly on one shoulder, and opened a box of raisins. I remembered something from my parenting books and started talking to Haley about what we'd do when we got home. She walked along beside the cart, munching her raisins and listening, appeased for the moment. I considered whether to go on or to just admit defeat and go home.

As I resumed the search for the restroom, still singing feebly, another shopper passed, a woman about ten years older than I, dressed in a stylish business suit and sporting a perfect manicure. I felt like a slug. She smiled as she passed and said, "Those are two lucky little girls."

I can't tell you how her words bolstered me. They felt like a shot of vitamins and a good night's sleep all in one. *She's right,* I thought. *I'm doing the best I can. I am a good mother!* Just to know that someone understood how hard I was trying and how tired I was—maybe that was all I needed. In six words, she'd said so much. She'd given me permission to be human, to stop trying to be super mom, and to stop beating myself up when I couldn't do it all. She knew I didn't have a clue how to pull this off, but in her few words and with her smile, she'd said that she'd been where I was and had survived—and she knew I could do it, too. We were sisters in this sacred vocation called motherhood. I wasn't as alone as I'd thought I was.

I won't say the next two hours were easy. We made three trips to the restroom for diaper changes and one more to breastfeed Molly. The ice cream melted before we got to the check-out. Haley cried a few more times, and I pulled Mama's singing trick again to calm us both. But I managed to buy most of what I set out for, and when we got home, we all took a nice, long nap.

I wish I knew who that other shopper was. I wish I could thank her for reaching out to an exhausted, overwhelmed, insecure new mom, for saying just the words I needed to hear just when I needed to hear them.

I'm shopping with four kids now, and I still have days when I wonder whether I can put one foot in front of the other. More often, though, I find myself looking for another frazzled mom in the store, the doctor's office, or the dry cleaner's who just needs to hear that she's not alone, that someone understands how frustrated and worn-out and guilty she feels. I try to give her permission to be human. Who knows? Today, it might be me lifting someone else up with a smile and a few encouraging words. Tomorrow, I might be the one wandering the aisles in a daze, and the words of another passing mom might be just the lifeline I need to stay afloat until my mom battery is recharged again.

Mimi Greenwood Knight

The Best-Laid Plans

I had it all figured out. Once I had confirmed the test results at the doctor's office, I knew I would be a great success at carrying and delivering a baby. I was already reading several books about the natural process of childbirth. I was so confident my body could handle this beautiful, organic experience that I proudly pursued a midwife and natural childbirth classes. My plans were only slightly derailed when my husband was transferred across the country, but I quickly found a new doctor who subscribed to my theories.

We went to our Lamaze classes, practiced our breathing at home, and signed up for a diaper service (I was ready to save the environment, too!). I was going to be super-granola-breastfeeding earth mama. Aside from the forty-pound weight gain and morning sickness that never really went away, my first pregnancy was free of complications. My doctor ordered an ultrasound two weeks before my due date, however, to determine just how large my little boy might be. My friends were now referring to me as a pregnant pencil. Every ounce of weight was concentrated to my midsection. My husband could actually rest his coffee cup on my stomach as he read the paper.

As the technician ran his wand across the great expanse of land otherwise known as my belly, I could not help but notice a confused look on his face.

"Is everything all right?" I whispered. My husband held my hand in anticipation.

"The baby looks just fine," the technician said. "He's a bit large—nine pounds, one ounce—but he is positioned in what we call footling breach. The umbilical cord also seems to be wrapped around his foot."

It was then, on the screen, that we could see our son sitting straight up, hands folded across his chest, with his legs in the lotus position (our perfect yoga baby).

"There is no way you can deliver this baby vaginally," the tech said with a laugh.

"Well, my doctor can just perform an inversion," I said with great mother-knowledge.

The tech guy grinned as only those in the baby business can. To this day I remember that grin. He was trying to be gracious and kind to a new mom who had precious plans she could not see past—plans that were admirable and good, but under the circumstances, irrelevant. "Inversion?" he gasped. "I'm no doctor, but there's no room to turn this baby around. He's taking up every inch of space you have." (Hence, the pregnant-pencil effect.) "Besides, no one would dare flip a baby over with the umbilical cord wrapped around his foot like that. We're talking dangerous here. I'm sending these results right over to your OB. Looks like someone is scheduling a c-section today."

When my doctor called, he confirmed all that the technician had to say, and there went my best-laid plans.

Henry was born one week later (as scheduled) at 8:37 A.M. My husband and I wore matching blue shower caps. I was witness to nothing, being flat on my back and behind a giant blue curtain, and yet, I remember every detail. After all of my preconceived notions of how a birth should take place, I would not want to remember what we experienced any differently. It may not sound beautiful to remember the feeling of someone tugging your child feet first from your abdomen, but it is a sensation I will never forget. It remains uniquely mine. My normally squeamish husband found himself captivated and in awe of the doctors working so delicately to aid my body in this process and to protect the precious life inside me. I can now share with him how it felt, and he shares with me what it all looked like. He heard the doctor whisper, "I see a foot," and then saw them pull slowly as they gingerly untangled the cord.

Henry's first touch of the air we breathe was not a desperate gasp from his lungs, but rather a gentle breeze across his ten perfect toes. Quickly, the nurses tended to him, and he soon began the cry new parents long to hear. The nurse brought him to me and held him close to my cheek. My newborn son and I gazed at each other as the tugging below continued, this time with a needle, thread, and staples to close the door that had been opened only for him. I wasn't the first to hold him, to see him, nor to comfort him, but I was the first to look at him with eyes that would behold him forever. My best-laid plans for childbirth had been replaced with ones I'd never expected. Now, it was time to bring baby home.

Cloth diapers can be a bit tricky post-op. There's something about those sticky safety pins not holding them in place correctly that requires an extra minute or two of standing, leaning over, and fussing. Those disposables, on the other hand, seem to slip right on. I hadn't really calculated how uncomfortable standing and fussing after a c-section might be. It was finally through the persuasion of my mother that I gave up on the diaper service. Finally, I could change a diaper quickly without bursting into tears.

Breastfeeding, though, was not an area on which I would compromise. Once again, I knew what was best. It actually went very well until I noticed our entire life was revolving around my breasts. Slowly, over time, I began to understand that my breastmilk was only one portion of Henry's needs. He also needed a happy, well-adjusted mom. My best-laid plans—the natural birth, the organic diapers, breastfeeding into the toddler years—had all been replaced with two sincere but limited parents and a beautiful child.

Enter pregnancy number two. My doctor assured me I would get that birth experience that had eluded me the first time. He said footling breaches were very rare. Well, I must be some rare breed, because Phoebe refused to flip over and was delivered just like her brother. It was like a beautiful trip down memory lane, only this time with a new prize. We had the chance to do it all again—the blue hats, the scrubs, the machines, the music of the IV drip flooding my veins, and that indescribable tug of life pulling a miracle from my insides. All these clinical, medicinal, highly technical devices were like flowers for a ceremony commemorating the birth of our first and announcing the arrival of our second. I know it all sounds crazy, but a new baby can make even an operating room seem romantic.

The blessing of the second time around was that there were no best-laid plans on my part. I simply did the best I could. I was able to see that I had been so determined with my first child to do it "my way" that I had gotten in the way of what was to be my son's own birth story. I learned that our stories tend to write themselves, whether or not we follow along as each page is being written.

I am so grateful to have done this twice. By the time we brought our daughter home, I was ready to simply be aware of all that was going on around me. I could appreciate our healthy newborn and admire our toddler as he worked hard to adjust to a growing family. The way they were born, the diapers they wore, whether they nursed or were fed formula all seems incidental now. So what if they preferred to enter the world feet first? Maybe it's an indication of their refusal to conform (I like to look at it that way when they don't listen to me). Whatever the reason, I consider their births to be layered insights into some of life's most valuable lessons.

I'm usually reticent to embrace clichés about God, but I'm quite fond of the following: "If you want to make God laugh, tell him your plans." If that one's true, I think I made the headlines in heaven the first time I became a new mom.

Shawn Daywalt-Lutz

More Than Words

Early arrivals can make for long waits. Such is the paradoxical world of premature babies. They rush into your life so far ahead of your well-tuned schedule that, by the time you've scrambled into position to receive them, all you can do is wait. With anxious heart and empty arms, you wait.

I should have known that something was askew on that bright, cloudless October day when an uncontrollable impulse—otherwise known as "the Nesting Urge"—ambushed me. I should have known, because this was my second baby and because my due date was more than two months away. But I succumbed unsuspectingly and set off for the local discount store to stock up on newborn disposable diapers. Later that afternoon, while my toddler slept, I washed the infant sleepers and prepared the bassinet. In retrospect, I should have known.

By four o'clock the next morning, I did know—something was terribly wrong. Bad abdominal cramping awakened me, and my bed sheets were damp. I tried to convince myself that this was a false alarm, that somehow everything would be all right.

My hands shook as I dialed my obstetrician's number, thoughts racing through my mind. *This can't be labor. It's too early. I'm not ready. Surely there's some way to stop the cramping, some pill, something!*

By then, my husband was awake, and he listened intently as I described my symptoms over the phone. My heart pounded as I waited for my doctor's reply.

"You need to come in," he said.

"Right away?" I shut my eyes and wished with all my will this wasn't happening.

"Yes. To the emergency room. As soon as you can." The urgency of his tone disintegrated any hopes I had of false alarms.

My husband and I moved like automatons on fast-forward in the stark chill of those predawn hours, our apprehension and fear disguised by curt declarations.

"I'll pack my bag."

"I'll call the Harpers to watch Elizabeth."

"Don't forget her diaper bag. Put in some extra clothes and diapers."

The doctor met us at the hospital, thirty miles away. Apprised of our situation, the medical staff attended to me swiftly while my husband filled out forms. A pelvic exam determined that my labor was past the point of no return.

It was no false alarm. I would not return home. Worse, Dr. Murray delivered his sobering assessment: our baby had a fifty-fifty chance of survival. I prayed. I hoped. I refused to dwell on those odds.

For the next fourteen hours, modern medicine did all it could to arrest my labor, but nature won out. By late evening, our son was born.

Thick tension cloaked the entire delivery room. Silence echoed off the walls.

And then, thin as butterfly wings, a cry. Relief washed through me. Nurses smiled. My husband squeezed my hand. We caught a brief glimpse of our tiny son before he was whisked away in what struck me as a plastic coffin. I was not allowed to hold him or even to touch his miniature hands. But at least our baby was alive . . . for now.

Dr. Murray had warned us that the first twenty-four hours were the most critical for premature infants. With an anxious heart and empty arms, I waited.

By midmorning the next day, the Demerol-induced fog I'd drifted in and out of all night had cleared and lucidity had returned. When Dr. Murray stopped in, he calmed my fears; my baby had made it through the night.

"Can I see him?" My heart yearned for it.

"Yes." He nodded slowly, and then updated me on my son's condition, summarizing his earlier conference with the neonatologist. "Just to warn you, he's on a respirator until he can breathe fully on his own. The sooner that happens, the better."

Tears welled in my eyes. Such a precarious word, "until."

"And until he gains strength, you won't be able to hold him." He explained how touch overstimulates a preemie and zaps the infant's small energy reserves, reserves crucial to survival.

Two tears escaped.

"I know this is hard on you," the doctor said. "I'm sorry." He gave my shoulder a gentle squeeze and left.

At that moment I felt a thousand different emotions tumbling inside me: gratitude, fear, sadness, worry, dread. He was alive, but how strong was he? Was he in pain? How long and how hard could he fight for life? Most of all, I felt a deep love for the son I'd given birth to just hours ago and longed to hold in my arms.

I pushed the call button. It was time to visit my baby boy. A nurse transported me down two floors in a wheelchair and through long hallways filled with cold fluorescent lights and the pungent odor of anti-septic. We stopped in front of a gray metal door, its small square window a cyclopean feature. The sign above it read "Neonatal Intensive Care Unit." I knew I sat at the threshold of a different world. No wide glass panels revealed rows of cherubic newborns bundled in soft cotton blankets. No proud parents or grinning grandmothers stood to coo over their new-est arrival. No spirit of celebration reigned here, only a specter of attenuated hope.

On the other side of the door, the charge nurse greeted us and briefly explained the visitation policy. While I sanitized my hands and donned gown, mask, and paper booties, she introduced me to my son's pri-mary-care nurse, Susan, a woman a little older than I with kind, brown eyes.

I made it through the pleasantries just fine. But when Susan rolled me into the main area of the NICU, the callous, unwelcoming reality of it shook me. Tubes, hoses, flashing lights, beeping monitors, wheezing respirators, and rows of doll-sized infants entombed in plastic cases—all of it assaulted my maternal instincts. I wanted to jump up and res-cue my baby from this artificial womb, to have him know the comfort of my loving arms, not this sterile existence.

I blinked back tears. I heard Susan's voice, but none of her words registered until we stopped by a multitiered infant warmer.

"Here he is," she said, her voice soft, as if to cushion the blow of what I'd see.

My newborn son, all three and a half pounds of bold but struggling surprise, lay tummy-down on a slim mattress surrounded by short Plexiglas sides. Overhead, a shiny metal arm emitted bright, warming light onto him. Several tubes and wires extended like tentacles from his splayed body, the largest one a respirator tube that was taped to his mouth and whooshed rhythmically.

My baby had the body of a skinny old man. His paper-thin skin read like a highly detailed metropolitan map, blue veins and capillaries exquisitely visible. His legs were thinly muscled and subtly defined. Wispy curls of dark hair covered his head, but this singular touch of beauty was marred by the unsightly wire of a parietal scalp monitor.

Without thinking, I reached out to touch him. My hand stopped in midair.

Tears flowed freely then, and I began to sob quietly. There was nothing I could do for my sweet, fragile baby. I couldn't hold him, I couldn't nurse him, I couldn't shower him with kisses. I felt so utterly helpless, so unlike a mother.

Susan tenderly patted my shoulder and waited until my anguish subsided.

"It hurts so much not to touch him," I whispered.

"This is always the hardest part. Even though you can't touch him, you can talk to him. He knows your voice, and he needs to hear it. It's his connection to you." Two more pats. "I'll leave you two alone for a while."

I realized that Susan was right. I had to offer my baby what I could. In an environment where machines were his constant company, my son needed to hear a human voice, especially his mother's. I wiped my nose one last time and leaned toward the warmer.

The respirator wheezed. The monitors beeped. And I talked.

Tears nearly choked back the words at first, but soon my normal tone took hold. I told my baby how much his mommy and daddy loved him. I told him about his big sister and his home and how many people cared about him and were praying for him.

When Susan returned an hour later, the flow of words had not stopped. I felt so much better. My arms were still empty, but my heart was no longer anxious.

From that point on, my general despondency lightened, and I grew into my new role as mother of a preemie. I learned how to use an electric breast pump so my baby could receive my milk through his feeding tube. I entrusted care of my daughter to generous friends so I could make daily visits to the hospital. And I cultivated friendships with my son's primary-care nurses, who acted as his guardian angels in my absence.

Yes, there were setbacks. His silent screams during necessary procedures. Being put back on the respirator for a short while. The way his tiny heels looked like overused pincushions from so many needle sticks to draw blood. But, for the most part, his condition progressed over several weeks. He was moved to an Isolette. The hospital staff brought his jaundice under control. He gained strength and weight.

Meanwhile, at his bedside, I never stopped talking to him.

At the end of the fourth week, the big moment arrived: I was allowed to hold my baby boy. On the Sunday following Thanksgiving, I sat in a large, wooden rocking chair, dressed in a fresh gown, my hands sanitized. My husband stood by my side and watched as Susan gingerly removed our son from the Isolette and laid him in my arms.

I had waited so long. I stroked his curly hair tenderly. Kissed his forehead gently. Held his still-miniature hand lightly.

And talked to him quietly.

As I caressed him with my words, I thought of how many ways there are to love a newborn. Touch is only one of them.

Ann Friesen

Ripple Effect

This is a story about what didn't happen at my son's birth. This is about the connection of one life to many others. This is a story for you, Dr. Patty Robertson, OB/GYN. You cannot know how the actions you took one April morning twenty-four years ago have affected the health and well-being of countless people.

Jacques, the child you delivered that day, is now an engineer who graduated from a top school. He is part of a team that designs insulin pumps; he makes them smaller and more reliable. All over the world, people with diabetes live longer and better because of the high-level critical and creative thinking that he contributes. And you, Dr. Patty, are the hidden member of his team, a person he doesn't even know. You played a major role in his birth, and as a result, you helped him in the work he does today. Because of your swift and courageous actions, Jacques survived his rocky entry into this world. Back then, you made a choice that gave him the gift of his mind, complete and intact. Now he uses that gift to help others.

Dr. Patty Robertson was one of five physicians, all women, in rotation at the OB/GYN practice that my husband Lou and I had chosen for the birth of our first child. It was the kind of office where the doctors encouraged patients to call them by their first names. In this less formal atmosphere, Patty's reassuring and easygoing manner made her a favorite among the patients. But at the time, I had no idea she would figure so largely in my son's outcome and future.

The pregnancy was not easy. Some time during my fifth month, I went into preterm labor and ended up in the hospital. Strong drugs slowed the contractions, but I went to bed and stayed there for the following four months, eating all my meals propped on my side and getting up only to visit the bathroom and drive to my doctors for a weekly checkup.

Bed rest was onerous but vital to sustain my pregnancy. If I had any doubts about lying in bed, they were erased when, just two days after the doctors deemed it safe for me to get up, I went into active labor.

Lou and I arrived at the hospital in the middle of the night. We had arranged for a birthing suite instead of the standard hospital room. The tiny room featured a rocking chair, a shower, paintings on the walls, and a regular bed rather than a delivery table. But by morning, I didn't care where I was. I was focused inward, as relentless contractions marked the passing hours. Because the baby's head was pressing against my spine, I was never out of pain, even between contractions. This condition went by the understated term "back labor" and the excruciating pain was described as "discomfort." Between that and the fact that I was weak from four months in bed, the night was a long haul.

Beyond the "discomfort," my greater concern was that I'd be given another label: "failure to progress." Failure to progress could lead to drugs that might domino into complicated surgical procedures. I was well aware of how slowly the all-important dilation number was increasing. When I had arrived at the hospital, my cervix was 5 centimeters dilated. Every time I was examined, my husband and I held hands, waiting for the number that would be closer to the golden 10 centimeters, indicating enough width for the baby to be born—and the cue for the final stage, when I could push. Throughout the long nighttime hours, I was stuck between 6 and 7.

As the sun rose outside the hospital window, Dr. Patty breezed into the room on the shift change. Despite her soft voice and the sweet smile on her round face, she energized the room, directing me into active management mode. I got out of bed and walked the long hallways, allowing gravity to work for me, leaning on Lou each time a contraction hit. I took a shower, the hot water pounding on my back to relieve some of the pain. My husband got soaked as I clung to him through more waves of contractions.

An hour later, I climbed back into bed, a pile of pillows behind my back propping me upright. Patty sat on the mattress next to my knees, cheering me through every surge, more like a midwife than a doctor. Finally, she broke my water and we roared through the next contractions like a freight train rounding the bend—all the way to 10! I could finally push.

With Patty's coaching, I quickly figured out how to add my conscious effort to what my body already knew how to do instinctively. My baby had a monitor on his head, giving us another set of numbers to go by. The machine, crowded near Lou next to the bed, glowed with the baby's oxygen levels. The number would drop down when I pushed and bounce back up in between contractions.

After two hours of pushing, the baby had moved into the birth canal but no farther. I was tiring fast. Patty handed me an oxygen mask so that my breathing would bring more air to the baby through the vital lifeline of his umbilical cord. I didn't know how much more I could do. This was a marathon, and the finish line was receding in the distance.

Then the oxygen levels on the machine went down with a contraction but didn't bounce back up when it subsided. A look of concern passed over my doctor's face. The baby's head had not crowned yet but was pressing hard, stretching my perineum, so I didn't feel the quick cut she made with the scalpel. She performed the episiotomy with one fast, smooth move and slipped her hand in next to my son's head. She told me what her fingers discovered: the cord wrapped tight in a loop around his neck—too short and with no way to loosen it. He could not be born vaginally like that. Any movement forward would constrict the cord even more, with less oxygen for him. And if the placenta prematurely pulled away from the uterine wall, the result could be a life-threatening hemorrhage for me.

Patty had to decide quickly. A cesarean would pull my baby back up, out of the birth canal, but would require a preparation time of twenty minutes. Twenty minutes of lower oxygen levels. Twenty minutes of oxygen starvation. He probably wouldn't die, but his brain would be compromised.

Her decision made within seconds, my doctor maneuvered the blunt-ended surgical scissors inside me, right around my son's head. She cut the lifeline cord. With that move, he had no more oxygen.

"Now," she commanded, "*push!*"

With that single word, the force of her will carried me forward. I sat almost upright and bore down once more. Jacques slid smoothly onto the bed, blue-skinned but with wide-open eyes, alert and blinking in the sun that poured through the window. He didn't cry. Everyone else did.

At my six-week checkup, cradling my infant son, I thanked Patty for that daring move.

"Wouldn't it have been well within medical procedure to do the cesarean?" I asked.

She told me that her own child had been born by surgery, and she always tried to avoid it if she could.

"But how did you know I'd be able to actually deliver him after his cord was cut? What if I'd given up?"

Patty laughed. "I was betting on you," she said. "Anyone who could push that hard for two hours—I knew you could do it."

I hadn't known I could do it. But her bet paid off.

It's not often you witness a single defining moment in which the culmination of clear thought and swift bravery determines the course of a life. Today, Jacques uses all the brains he was born with, designing medical equipment that helps thousands of others live better. So thank you, Patty Robertson. Your calculated risk twenty-four years ago was like the stone thrown into still water. Your decisive action has rippled outward, affecting Jacques, his family, and many others you will never meet.

Sometimes the best stories are about what didn't happen.

Mary-Kate Mackey

Tooth by Tooth

The day begins before I am ready, at 5:54 A.M., when a puddle of guacamole escapes my daughter's diaper and runs down my leg to settle on the sheet, seeping through to the mattress. I quickly fling our quilt away from the mess and lay there collecting my thoughts. Emily is asleep, her head resting on my stomach, and I am reluctant to wake her, but she needs a new diaper. I reach over to shake her father awake, but there is a mountain of laundry in the place where he usually sleeps. I'd meant to finish folding and putting it away last night after nursing the baby to sleep, but apparently I'd fallen asleep too. He must have slept on the couch. No sense in waking him for this, anyway; he had come home late, and besides, I can handle this. I tuck her sweaty body under one arm and climb over the pile of laundry, feeling a bit like King Kong carrying Fay Wray up the skyscraper.

Her diaper goes in another pile, ripe for the wash. They will have to get in line behind the towels, which are in line behind his work clothes, which sit in the dryer, gathering wrinkles. *We're not getting any younger in here,* they mock.

Put a sock in it. Now I am talking to laundry.

My daughter unleashes a fresh stream of digested milk onto the changing pad. One less diaper to wash, I reason, as I throw the pad onto the pile as well.

When Emily is clean, I bring her to the couch and lay her down beside her father.

"Please, while I shower?"

We speak in shorthand these days.

"She blew out the bed and my leg; I need a rinse."

He sits up partway, still mostly asleep, "Hmm, okay."

As I head to the bathroom, she begins to cry. Her daddy tries to comfort her, but the crying gets louder and louder, following me into the bathroom, out of my pajamas, and into the palm of my hand as I test the water temperature. I stare at it numbly for a long moment, turn off the faucet, and return to my daughter.

"Sorry, Daddy," I mumble. "Didn't know she was hungry."

Emily nurses as I rock her. Our bare bellies press together. She flashes me her toothless grin, which will soon disappear forever, tooth by tooth. I can already see the white seeds pressing against the surface of her gums. There are so many things I will miss, so many I already miss. Her soft, breathy voice sighing along with the lullaby I have sung to her since she was an island rising out of the bathwater has been replaced with cackling and high-pitched screams of delight. In place of the small handful of flesh that squeaked like a new puppy and rooted for milk, I now cradle a growing baby who laughs and blows spit bubbles until she appears rabid.

I buckle Emily into the bouncy chair, and she squeals happily when it starts vibrating. She will work on ripping the plastic elephant down from its Velcro, while I wash off my leg.

The shower feels so good that I wash the spit-up out of my hair and even use shampoo. By the time I get out and wring a drop of toothpaste out of the tube, the baby is bored and crying again. Flossing is a luxury that I cannot afford this morning. There is nowhere to sleep, but she and I are both desperate, so we squeeze in at the foot of the bed, between the laundry and the mess. I can't wash the sheet until the laundry is folded, and I can't fold the laundry until my daughter and I get some more rest. So we sleep.

We wake up, refreshed, a few hours later. Sunlight dapples the bed, and the wind outside conducts an orchestra of rustling leaves, all clamoring to be heard. Her daddy is up, neatly folding and putting away the clothes from the bed. I can hear the dryer humming and the washer washing. This is a beautiful scene, and yet, somehow, the arguing begins almost immediately.

I want him to take the baby for an hour so I can write, and he wants to relax before going to work. I convince him to take her by promising breakfast. The pancakes tear, and the yolks break, and the sausage burns. The baby fusses, and we trade, spatula for child.

"Just cut some avocado, and it's ready."

I try to nurse Emily some more, but she doesn't want to nurse. She doesn't want a pacifier. She will take only fingers. Somehow, I manage to eat with one finger in her mouth and my other arm under her body. It seems akin to spoon bending, and yet I am the only one who notices. After breakfast, I buckle her into the bouncy seat again, this time so I can finish folding the laundry. She rubs her feet back and forth and starts whimpering right away. Daddy picks her up and takes her to the changing pad, then tosses me the final straw.

"It must be so nice to just lie around nursing all day. I don't have that luxury, because I have to work."

I throw down whatever I had been folding and storm away.

"Wait, I'm sorry, where are you going?"

"Taking a break!" I yell back. "I just need a break!"

I climb up to the attic and sit in the corner with my books. The air is thick and hot up here. I drop to the floor and stare at the titles. I remember studying up here, before my brain turned to mush and my belly got too large to stoop under the low ceiling. Before having a baby, I took everything for granted: the ability to leave the house on a whim, to ride a bike, to go swimming, to finish writing a sentence. Most of all, I took my own mother for granted. I'd had no idea. Now, I just want her like my daughter wants me.

I go back downstairs and pick up my daughter. I call my mother and ask if she can drive down to visit soon. She can't this weekend but promises soon.

"It sounds like you need a break," she says. "Maybe you can come up here."

She offers to buy me a train ticket, and by the time we hang up, I feel okay again. Somehow, after all these years, she is still able to make it better.

My daughter and I go outside and sit on the porch. Dandelion seeds dance past us on the breeze. The cats are stalking one another and wrestling in the tall grass. Emily sits in her little blue seat while I knit a few rows. I am making a cat doll for her, white with orange stripes. It will look just like one of our cats, but right now it's just a square patch. She watches carefully as I pull the stitches through, one by one. I realize that our lives are a bit like this: as the moments line up, each connects to the other in an imperceptible pattern until our lives take on a new form. Just like the strands of yarn twisting around each other will eventually become a cat, Emily and her father and I are weaving our new selves into the shape of a family, made up of all these moments. As long as we remember to put love in the stitches, our family will grow stronger every day, becoming something wonderful we could never have foreseen, even if we are sometimes frayed at the ends.

Kendal Seager

Where's a New Mother to Turn?

I was a competent and independent woman. I graduated college as valedictorian. I worked successfully in various fields. I managed to carry on satisfying and healthy relationships. Then I had a baby. My transition to motherhood was, shall we say, bumpy. I was a wreck. Though I didn't stay that way—not completely, anyway—at the time it felt like I would. I was certain I would be sitting on the couch, bleary-eyed, in a dirty shirt, for the rest of my life. I was completely intimidated by this tiny dictator who screamed at me for reasons I couldn't figure out. I've never been more desperate for advice. I was receptive, ready to listen. Calling all know-it-alls! Bring it on. I was a dream audience. I was a sponge. But, believe it or not, I found amazingly few takers.

Of course, instinct led me directly to my mother. But to every inquiry, from breastfeeding to diaper rash, I got pretty much the same response.

"Sweetie, the last time I had a baby was thirty-six years ago."

Mom's response was not only no help, it was a fresh little reminder of how late I'd come to mothering and how I probably had no business doing so at my age.

My obstetrician seemed like the next most likely candidate to query, but forget that. She barely had time to rush into the delivery room to catch my son before he hit the floor. I was fairly certain there would be no postnatal advice from her, unless my insurance policy covered it and I booked the appointment to ask three months in advance.

I had a midwife. She kept giving me vile-tasting tea to drink and telling me to write encouraging messages to myself on the bathroom mirror and the kitchen window. She would talk to me through my son.

"Tell your mommy she just needs to visualize big, wide, rushing rivers of milk for you."

This was not helpful. She wasn't completely useless, however. One day she gave me a foot rub, charging it to my insurance as a postnatal follow-up. Now you're talking!

My son had a pediatrician. She was French, which you can't fault her for, since we lived in France. I regularly phoned or rushed into her office in a panic. She would assume a certain knowing, and somewhat patronizing, smile. I could hear it even over the phone. Then she would utter her favorite, and apparently only, words of wisdom. *"Bah, oui—c'est ca."* Roughly translated, "Yep."

One morning, while visiting with my boss, I hallucinated the Loch Ness monster in my coffee cup. My boss was an experienced father of two. Perhaps he could tell me how to persuade my child to sleep. I got a bit weepy while asking, "Will I ever have a night's sleep again, ever, for the rest of my life, which won't be very long if I don't get some damned sleep?"

He suddenly beamed with what can only be described as a sadistic grin and replied in this voice that was, well, a bit nasty. "I just *love* watching brand -new parents."

My misery had made his day. He's from Brooklyn. I should've known better than to fish in his pond for sympathy.

There was another mother in my apartment building whose daughter was six months older than my son. You'd think that would qualify her as my main mentor. From her I got one of two answers.

"Oh yes, Lauren went through that. I didn't know what to do about it, either." This was always followed by a sigh, which meant, *Thank God we're done with that; poor you, still stuck there.* Her alternate response was, "Hmmm. No, Lauren never did that," after which there was simply nothing more to say.

I tried a mommy group. We mothers would sit around holding our coffee cups aloft and blurting out sentence fragments about diapers and teething, while our babies and toddlers generated mayhem on all sides. Whenever a conversation came dangerously close to being honest or interesting, one of "those" women would rise up and shame us all into retreating back behind our "together" masks.

"Those" women are the ones who "just loved being pregnant." They respond to all whimpering with a deep sigh, a contented smile, and "Oh, but it's so worth it, isn't it?"

Good grief. What can you say after that? Of course, it's worth it. No one said it wasn't worth it. We love our kids more than a day at the spa. We'd give them the air out of our lungs. But don't we all have moments, if not days, when we question the wisdom of continuing the human race? How can you say that to some woman who wore her favorite skinny jeans home from the hospital?

One evening I ended up in an impromptu conversation with a friend who had just had her third child. She talked about months of panic attacks and hysteria after her first baby was born. We laughed together about the constant chorus of voices saying, "Enjoy it while he's small. It goes so fast."

Enjoy it? I'm not sure I'll survive it! And as for going fast, come tell me that at 2:00 A.M. and 3:00 A.M. and 4:00 A.M.! Something about my friend's honesty, contrasted with her current aura of peace and calm, gave me hope and brought sanctuary into my soul.

I went home and threw away all but two of the mountain of books citing fifty-seven different opinions on the same question. I stopped clawing for advice and began trusting my own instincts as a mother. Looking back, although I often felt stranded on a stormy sea, I realized that each person to whom I had turned had been a life preserver just by their presence and their love. Once my desperation passed, I deeply appreciated and enjoyed the people around me, especially my son.

Where's a new mother to turn? Anywhere. Everywhere. Just keep turning. No one will provide all the answers or pluck you out of the stormy sea, but in continuing to embrace every small scrap of support offered, you will one day find yourself safely on the shore and this amazing little person will be by your side. And that bit everyone tells you about the second one being so much easier? I found it to be true.

Kristi Hemingway

Imperfect, Not Incompetent

I laid my screaming five-month-old son in his crib. Closing the bedroom door behind me to muffle his cries, I headed out to the front porch to get a breath of sanity.

Lack of sleep and a surplus of frustration made my eyes burn. I had changed my son's diaper, nursed him, and rocked him. Just as I'd laid him down, he'd begun to cry again—for the third time.

Overwhelmed by self-doubt, I squeezed my eyes shut as the tears trickled down my cheeks. What was wrong with me? Why couldn't I figure out how to calm my child? Why wouldn't he sleep? I was thirty-two years old and a first-time mother. A teacher by profession, I could handle a room of thirty-five ninth graders. Why was I so inept as the mother of an infant?

I checked my watch. I had been outside about two minutes. I wished that covering my ears would help, but I knew it wouldn't. I had recently read in a child-care book that if I felt like throwing my baby out a window, I should put him in a crib or safe environment and step outside for a few minutes. At the time, I thought, *What sane mother is going to feel like that?* Now I knew . . . me.

I rubbed my arms and inhaled slowly. The autumn air did calm me a bit. I checked my watch again. Three minutes. He was still crying. No, now he was wailing.

I began to pace the porch, but fatigue convinced me to go inside and lie down on the couch. My son continued his verbal attack on my qualifications for motherhood. I reminded myself of the reasons I shouldn't go pick him up.

The pediatrician had expressed no concern about Jeff's crying when I'd peppered him with questions: "How long should I let him cry?" "Won't he hurt himself?" "Shouldn't I comfort him?"

"He's testing you," he replied.

I said nothing.

"He's exercising his lungs. He needs to cry," the doctor added.

I'd left the office still feeling guilty. I worried all that crying could permanently scar my son's psyche.

I envisioned the tabloid headlines: *Crazed Killer Claims Crying Infants Ignite His Rage.*

I glanced at the clock on top of the entertainment center. Ten minutes. Jeff was still crying, but not as loudly.

Other mothers I knew cooed about the sleeping habits of their babies.

"Oh, she's been sleeping through the night since she was six weeks old," boasted one.

"I just put him in the crib, and he gurgles until he falls asleep," said another.

I had remained quiet, digging my nails into my palms. Concentrating on the pain in my palms masked the ache in my heart. It did not silence the voice in my head: *What's wrong with you?* it hissed.

Other matters troubled me, too. I grew bored with my son. The highlights of my day were his naptime and bedtime. I didn't record each ounce he gained in the baby book. I didn't remember the date he first smiled. *Was I a bad mother?* I fretted.

Several women I knew moaned about how quickly their infants were growing. "I love them when they're so small and helpless," said one.

I thought, *I can't wait until he can entertain himself. I long for the day he can tell me what's wrong and why he can't sleep.*

Deciding to stay at home rather than continuing to work amplified my frustration. As a teacher, I exuded confidence and efficiency in the classroom. Both supervisors and parents complimented me on my skills. Many of my students confessed, "I used to hate English, but I like your class."

Mothering, on the other hand, baffled me. Some days I felt like an unwilling participant in a bizarre psychological experiment: *Trapped in an empty class-room with a wolf cub, I read the instructions scrawled on the chalkboard: "Teach the cub to diagram sentences. Then we'll set you free." The wolf howls. I can't even find a piece of chalk.*

Unfortunately, nothing could have prepared me adequately for the 24/7 motherhood marathon. No matter how difficult a day had been at work, at least I had the satisfaction of closing my classroom door and going home. No matter how obnoxious a student was, at the end of the day he boarded a bus that took him far, far away. No commute carried me to a haven of solitude now; no bus rumbled down the street, taking my wailing infant with it.

Caring for a baby also required random pin-the-tail-on-the-donkey techniques that conflicted with the rational discipline methods I used at school. I could not strap my son into his high chair and explain how his disruptive behavior destroyed the equilibrium of our home. Neither could I post on a chalkboard the specific behavior patterns that would improve our rapport.

One day I finally confessed to a friend, whose children were teenagers, that I was not enjoying my son's infancy.

She chuckled and admitted, "Neither did I."

"Really?" I wanted to grab her and dance a jig, but I just sighed in relief.

"Really," she said. "Not every woman enjoys babies. I like my kids much better now that they're teens."

At that moment, the neon sign flashing "Incompetent Mother" over my head crashed to the ground. Of course, my son did not suddenly begin to sleep better. He continued to cry himself to sleep at naptime and bedtime until he was thirteen months old. However, I did stop blaming myself for his poor sleep habits.

I never savored the helpless, dependency stage of my children. Some mothers cry when their kids begin to walk and become mobile, willful toddlers. I celebrated my children's independence, knowing that intelligible dialogue would soon follow.

As the years passed, my tendency to push my kids toward self-sufficiency became an asset rather than a liability. I encouraged them to take risks. I told my daughter, "Go ahead. Sign up for softball. You'll have fun with your friends." I also prodded them to solve their conflicts with peers. "Don't whine. Tell Nate you're sorry. Play the game by his rules this time."

My son and his younger sister are both teenagers now. They survived infancy without a twelve-inch-thick baby book chronicling every burp. They weathered childhood, even though I never badgered a bus driver to change my child's seat or phoned a principal about a teacher's insensitive remark.

My teenagers talk to me. I consider that a merit badge on my motherhood sash. Sometimes when I'm reading at night, my daughter emerges from her bedroom. She drapes her leg over the arm of my chair and asks, "So how's life going for ya, Mom?" As I prepare dinner, my son occasionally lumbers into the kitchen and spreads his arms wide. "Come on, Mom, give me a hug!" he bellows.

I don't have perfect kids. They don't have a perfect mother. Somehow, though, our imperfections make us a perfect match.

Denise K. Loock

Taking Care

My husband tried to cushion the blow. "I swear I didn't encourage him at all, but Miles sort of took a couple of steps today," he said over the phone.

For a moment I couldn't speak. A lump rose in my throat. I had left my baby overnight for the first time in his ten months of life to attend a business conference out of town. There I was, in an overly air-conditioned hotel, dressed in a stiff new suit and shoes that pinched, while at home my son took his first steps. And I missed them.

I know, I know. I've heard all the reasoning. There will be plenty of other "firsts." I'd been there for all of them so far; let Dad have his turn. And it's not like Miles will remember or care that on the day he started walking, Mom was off collecting business cards.

As a new mom, I am discovering what every parent must eventually accept—that raising a child is an endless exercise in learning to let go. From giving up the warm security of the womb (after nineteen hours of labor) to going off to college (or joining a punk band), our offspring gradually gain their independence, whether we like it or not. Still, even leaving my baby for an hour while I got my teeth cleaned felt like a big deal in the beginning.

The first time I left my son with someone else was a few weeks after he was born. Since I had been living in a bathrobe with a baby attached to me for most of that time, I was dying to get dressed, put on some makeup, and rejoin the rest of the world. I didn't even know what was playing, but my parents convinced my husband and me to go out to a movie. At the theater, my head swirled along with the crowd around us. How strange and liberating to be part of normal life again. Honestly, I didn't miss my baby during those few hours. Besides, at that point I was convinced that he was far better off with his grandparents. At least they knew what they were doing. However, because I was his food supply, our separation didn't last long.

By the time Miles was three months old, I was itching to do something besides practice my swaddle technique and research strollers on the Internet. My brain felt as soft and unused as all those receiving blankets I'd been given at my baby shower. I work from home, so going back to work consisted of finding a babysitter and escaping to our home office for a few days a week. As luck would have it, the retired mother of a friend had just moved to town and was looking for a babysitting job. Her friendly charm and Southern accent instantly put me at ease. It was obvious she loved babies. Plus, she'd raised two of her own. She was more qualified than I was.

Even so, the first day Patricia came over to watch Miles, I bombarded her with instructions on how to hold him, burp him, change him, and feed him. I showed her how to make the bouncy seat vibrate and where the spare batteries were for the baby monitor. I carefully laid out Miles' favorite silky blanket, some extra pacifiers, and several changes of clothes. The sitter just smiled and bounced the baby on her hip.

Finally, I mustered up the courage to leave the house. I drove two blocks to a bagel shop and immediately checked my cell phone. No new messages. As I sat there sipping my lemonade and pretending to read the newspaper, I began to panic. What if she forgot how to heat up the baby's bottle? What if she didn't wash off his pacifier after he dropped it? Had I shown her where we keep the fire extinguisher? Did we even own a fire extinguisher? Gradually, I loosened the reins a bit. By Patricia's third month with us, I even left my cell phone in the car when I ran into the post office.

It was one thing to leave my baby for a few hours here and there. The next big step for me was leaving him for an entire day. Again, my parents offered to watch him, only this time I wasn't as sure of their skills. Miles was older, more active, and aware that Mom was ditching him to go out. His grandparents would need to feed him three meals, give him his bottles, put him down for naps, and most important, keep him from careening headfirst off the stairs. I wasn't convinced they were up to the task. But when I returned eight hours later, Miles was happily playing with measuring spoons in his high chair as his grandmother made dinner. He barely seemed to notice I'd been gone.

By the time I was finally ready to leave my baby overnight, I had more confidence in the caretaking ability of others. Besides, I was leaving him with his dad—the second most qualified person besides me, I thought smugly. Before I left, I carefully wrote out Miles' daily schedule and reminded my husband that baths and naps were not optional. Secretly, I hoped Miles might give him a taste of what my days were like. Anyone who thinks staying home with a baby is easy hasn't endured changing table wrestling matches, 101 ways to prepare sweet potatoes, and naps that barely last long enough for a shower. But, wouldn't you know it, the boys' weekend was one big party. They watched sports, played with the dog, and took long walks. The baby even napped for two hours straight one day—an unprecedented event.

I was finally forced to accept the lesson it had taken me ten months to learn. It turns out my baby can stay alive and happy when left in the care of others from time to time. And you know what? I benefited from those breaks, too. Each time, I came back refreshed and ready to embrace motherhood again. Diaper rash? Teething? Tantrums? Bring it on!

Of course, there were some mishaps along the way. When our sitter casually mentioned that she'd tucked Miles in for a nap with a blanket, terror seized my heart. I restrained myself from rattling off the latest SIDS statistics, and instead, managed to calmly inform her of the dangers of loose crib bedding. The day I left the baby with his grandmother, I came home to find the carefully premeasured milk still in the container. Apparently, she'd forgotten his afternoon bottle. She was more distraught than I was. As for Miles, I doubt the omission made even a dent in his dimpled thighs.

All those months, I was so concerned that no one else could take care of my baby as well as I could. Yet, the sitter, my parents, and my husband each returned Miles as happy and healthy as I'd left him. You could even say he thrived in their care. Patricia taught him to wave "bye-bye," his grand-mother got him to sit still for five minutes, and his dad encouraged Miles to take his first steps. (Make that "witnessed" his first steps.)

In any case, when I returned home that weekend, my son immediately demonstrated his new skill by lurching into my outstretched arms. Since then, he's gotten faster and more sure-footed by the day. More often than not he chases after the dog rather than me. I like to think I encouraged his independence by leaving him with trusted caretakers now and then. Not to mention, if I never left, I wouldn't have those welcome-home hugs to look forward to.

Abigail Green

For Crying Out Loud

What is wrong with my baby? I thought, as yet another family member thrust him into my arms after numerous attempts to calm him down. I hurriedly carried PJ upstairs to allow the family to continue their visit in peace.

Feelings of guilt, embarrassment, and shame overwhelmed me as I sunk further and further into what would soon be identified as postpartum depression. I longed for PJ's first visit to the pediatrician so I could inform her that the hospital had mistakenly given me the wrong baby. My baby was sweet and happy and loved to cuddle. I'm not sure whose baby I'd brought home, but I was intent on taking him back and demanding a refund.

To my dismay, the first visit to Doctor Lauren did little to allay my anxiety. That night, I lay in bed and stared at the copy of *What to Expect When You're*

Expecting on my bookshelf, thinking, *They should include a disclaimer that none of these so-called pearls of wisdom apply if you happen to have a baby with colic.*

So it was that my darling little PJ had what may have been the nastiest case of colic to ever grace the pages of medical journals. I reached this conclusion around the seventh time I heard the claim, "I have never seen a baby like this." After hours of futile conversation leading only to more questions and countless calls to the doctor to plead my case that something must be done, I convinced myself to accept the diagnosis and began the arduous journey of surviving the first few months of my newborn son's life.

Two weeks passed at a painfully slow pace, but at least the postpartum depression seemed to be running its course. Despite my apprehension, the antidepressants really were a necessity. I'd also discontinued nursing to help restore my physical health. My appetite returned, and at that point, my struggles were confined mostly to incessant teeth grinding and a lack of sleep, both of which I could manage.

PJ's colic, however, had complete control over almost every aspect of my life. I quickly became an expert on the matter and felt certain I could write a book. I fielded endless questions and tried tirelessly to convince others of the severity of the case, frustrated with good intentions that offered little solace. Though I recognized the need of others to "fix" the problem, I was certain if I heard the phrase, "Have you tried . . ." one more time, I would snap and hurl my frustration and rage at the closest innocent victim. I had, indeed, tried everything. I switched formula four times. I moved PJ from carrier to swing to stroller to bouncer to just about anything I could find that swayed or vibrated. I watched *The Happiest Baby on the Block* and tried all five of the S-techniques. I swaddled, side-lied, swayed, and shushed, and PJ sucked pacifier after pacifier. I soon realized that everything worked for about five minutes at a time—and that, during those brief moments, PJ was merely reloading for Round Two. I simply did not have the happiest baby on the block. In fact, I had the angriest baby. At least that's how I felt.

I was appalled by total strangers commenting on my failure to parent my child as they saw fit. One afternoon, as my husband, Grant, and I strolled around the harbor, seemingly oblivious to PJ's deafening cries, we passed a lady who exclaimed, "Oh, Mommy, do your job and feed him." It was all I could do to keep my clenched fists from finding their way to her accusing eyes. Perhaps I needed to be swaddled to contain my rage. Instead, I simply informed her that PJ had just been fed.

I could not convince others that I was not exaggerating, that PJ's colic really *was* "that bad." But one by one they fell, each, after spending hours with him during one of his "episodes," arriving at the same conclusion: "What is wrong with your baby?" I admit to being amused by the self-righteous spirit within me who whispered, *Told ya so!*

I also took great pleasure in watching family member after family member emerge from my son's room boasting, "He's asleep," as if they had the magic touch. Again, I smirked, knowing that PJ would be wide awake, kicking and wailing, in less than two minutes.

Getting my son to sleep was a science I affectionately referred to as "the dance." It entailed a precise rocking technique, firm grip to contain his flailing arms, and only when he let out a very shrill, loud squeak could we be sure he was entering deep sleep. It was then that we could safely place him in his crib and call it a night. The process took approximately an hour, sometimes two. He simply did not like to sleep and fought every urge to close his eyes as if he were going to miss something extraordinary. After several attempts to break free from his tightly wrapped blanket, he would finally just give in. I imagine he felt frustrated on more than one occasion. I could relate.

Even the new-mom support groups offered little more than cold coffee and free stroller parking. In fact, they seemed to only aggravate the frustration and intolerance building within me. I could not relate to the mothers whose biggest struggle was whether or not to swaddle. That decision had been made for me. PJ's arms and legs flailed so uncontrollably that we had no choice but to swaddle him to get him to sleep and to keep him from injuring himself. The task was further exacerbated by the fact that he was nearly ten pounds at birth, strong enough to hold his head up at two days old, and more alert than any baby I'd ever seen.

I took issue with the mothers who questioned how long to allow their babies to cry before they rushed to comfort them. PJ's longest episode lasted fourteen hours, and if I were to allow him to cry for even a brief moment, the inconsolable screams increased by the minute.

It was difficult to watch the other mothers smile and laugh with their babies. The nature of colic is such that it causes an overreaction to every stimulus, every emotion, and every physical change in a baby's body. I could not allow PJ to get too excited or to play too long for fear that it would bring on an episode.

Some of the new moms questioned how to get their babies to sleep longer at night. Again, unable to relate, I finally recognized the silver lining on the cloud of colic. The hours of daylight PJ spent fussing, fighting, and wearing himself out were eventually met with approximately eight hours of sleep at night to recover from the exhaustion. Yet, sometimes, even the restful hours were filled with fear and anxiety over when PJ would awaken. I would jokingly tell Grant, "Honey, I'm afraid of the baby."

I soon gave up on support groups, as they only affirmed my feelings of loneliness. What I needed was a support group for mothers of colicky babies, and there was none. I also needed a vacation, several shots of tequila, and an operation to have my tubes tied, but those would have to wait. In the meantime, I had no choice but to find the light at the end of the tunnel.

And so I learned. I learned that having a child should not be referred to as "expecting." At the very least, all parents should familiarize themselves with exactly what it is they are expecting. I was expecting a baby that cooed and giggled. PJ's coos were drowned out by the deafening cries of infant angst.

I learned that it is instinctual for others to assume that when a baby cries, he or she simply wants and needs its mother. I learned to accept that at times not even I could comfort my son and that, though it broke my heart, it did not make me insufficient or incompetent as his mother.

I learned that colic is defined as an immature nervous system, a condition for which no cure exists. It simply has to run its course, which typically lasts three to four months. Although, at first, I longed for the first few months to pass in the blink of an eye, I was blessed with the ability to recognize that I would then long to get that time back. So I learned to delight in every moment, even during the worst episodes, and to celebrate the highs and lows of motherhood. I soaked up brief moments of contentment and cherished the first few minutes when PJ first awoke, before his little mind remembered that he was not happy with his surroundings and his body responded accordingly.

My soul rejoiced when PJ learned to smile at six weeks old. His squeaks of enjoyment were music to my ears. I learned that there is no other PJ; he truly is unique, and I am unabashedly humbled by his presence in my life. I consider myself more than blessed to be his mommy. Someday, when PJ is older and I look back on this brief period of time in my life, I will smile and tell him there is one thing the experience of colic could not teach me.

One thing I did not need to learn was to love him with my whole heart, for I truly did love him from the beginning and will love him forever and ever.

Julie Sharp

Mirroring Mom

I held my two-month-old baby closely to my body as I moved my still ponderous postpregnancy bulk up the two steps to my bed. The arches of my feet ached, and the lower part of my stomach was sore from its recent trauma. Sitting on the edge of my bed, I swung one leg up onto the bed, followed by the other, and slowly inched my way back to the headboard; not an easy task to complete while holding an infant. I felt my weight shift uncomfortably as I settled back against my pillow to prepare to nurse my son. Remembering my once thinner body and feeling quite unattractive, I sighed.

At only five feet and a quarter inch tall (hey, that quarter inch is important!) and originally about 115 pounds, I had gained more than half my original body weight while pregnant and had given birth to a nine-pound, two-ounce boy. When I had given birth to my daughter, Mackenzie, I had been able to get back to my original weight, but that had been six years ago. I was well into my thirties now, and my metabolism had slowed down considerably. *Oh well,* I thought, *it was worth it, and hopefully I'll feel better about my body soon.*

Mackenzie had trailed after me into my bedroom, asking, "Is it time to feed Carter, Mommy?"

"Yep. Do you want to sit on the bed with us?" I asked.

"Okay," she answered cheerfully. She clambered up onto the bed, taking my husband's pillow and dragging it over to place it right next to my already propped-up one. She leaned her back against the pillow and, with a gentle sigh, snuggled up to my shoulder.

Mackenzie watched as I placed Carter's face close to my breast and guided him to begin his evening meal. All was quiet while Carter situated himself, the only sound his gentle breathing. Then suddenly, a proclamation from Mackenzie: "I'm going to feed my baby!"

"Uh, okay," I murmured to her retreating back as she raced out of my room and across the hall.

I could hear her rummaging in her bedroom for her doll of choice. After a few moments, she entered my room holding her "baby" triumphantly aloft. The fingers on her outstretched hand gripped the doll's neck and her feet were spread wide in a victorious stance. "I got her!" she announced. It was one of her favorites. The doll's body was cottony soft all over and clothed in pink and white. The stitched-on face was beige and surrounded by a white, doily-like attachment for a bonnet effect.

Mackenzie climbed up on the bed again, settling back into the spot she had previously arranged next to me. She brought her baby close to her body.

I had been expecting her to cradle the doll next to her chest and to rock her "baby" while I nursed Carter. Once again, my daughter caught me off guard. I watched as she lifted her shirt and let it rest on top of her baby's head while she guided her baby's face close to one side of her chest.

"Are you sure you don't want to just hold your baby?" I asked her, slightly uncomfortable with her imitating me to the last detail of my actions.

"No, this is what I want to do."

Mackenzie looked up at me with her chocolate eyes framed with dark lashes and her furrowed brow. My guilt at not allowing her to experiment compelled me to say, "All right, go ahead."

A few restless moments passed as Mackenzie kept moving her baby into various positions.

"Is everything okay?" I ventured to ask.

"She won't latch on!" Mackenzie complained. She had been paying more attention than I could have imagined.

"Don't worry, keep trying. She will soon," I advised, hiding a smile.

After a few more minutes of fussing, I received the next update.

"Oh, now she's eating."

We nursed our babies in companionable quiet for the next few moments.

Then suddenly, "Ouch! She bit me!" Mackenzie cried out.

This time, I had to actually turn my head away to hide my wide grin as I asked, "Oh my goodness, are you all right?" in a warbled voice unlike my own, due to the laugh lodged in my throat.

"Mommy, are you laughing?" (My daughter knows me.)

"No, I just need to cough." I coughed.

As we settled in for the final moments of nursing our babies, I gazed down at Carter, then over at Mackenzie, and felt a deep sense of fulfillment in being a mother. Yes, I was fat, flabby, and bloated from water retention. Yes, I will forever carry the bodily imprints of motherhood in the form of stretch marks and a cesarean-section scar. I was in no frame of mind to feel glamorous or sexy; in fact, my whole body hurt.

However, my insecurities about my weight and outside appearance receded a bit in priority as I recognized the importance of the here-and-now of motherhood. My daughter admired me and wanted to imitate what she saw as a natural aspect of motherhood; she saw a role model, not a lumbering bear of a mother.

Mackenzie had reminded me about my purpose in the journey of motherhood. Almost anybody can be thin with a relatively simple combination of motivation, diet, and exercise. Being a good mother takes infinitely more effort, dedication, and self-control. True motherhood means doing whatever is necessary to nurture and to protect my child. It means searching my soul to discover my own personal convictions and to examine my own actions, because I have the grave responsibility of being a positive example to easily influenced children who watch my every move and hear my every word.

My daughter and I finished our nursing session, straightened our shirts, and proceeded to carefully burp our babies. After burping successfully, we got off the bed, Mackenzie sliding carelessly down the side of the bed, while I gingerly stepped down the stool with Carter held tightly against my body. I followed Mackenzie as she skipped down the hallway, swinging her baby by her soft cotton hand. We made our way into the kitchen for a bedtime snack (nursing made us hungry).

Kristina J. Adams

Hello, Baby—Goodbye, Body

After giving birth to two babies not quite seventeen months apart, the physical transformation into motherhood has left my body in a state of disrepair.

Besides being out of shape, I have two very energetic little boybies occupying much of my time and a part-time job taking up most of the rest of it, so I often find myself too busy to eat right. Because I'm hypoglycemic, not eating right is very, very wrong. If I forget to eat, my blood sugar level plummets, resulting in headaches and dizziness. When this happens, I crave sugar and other white foods, which are usually categorized as "naughty" on any diet I've ever heard about. I try not to have cookies, chips, and such in the house, but if they happen to be there, they're not long for this world if I suddenly come up for air and realize I need to eat.

This probably explains, in part, why I haven't got my prepregnancy figure back yet.

People are just so encouraging: "It took nine months to get that way; give yourself nine months to get back."

Hello, everyone, it's been eight months, and I still look four months pregnant (according to the post office clerk)!

With my hectic new-mom life, it also has been hard to keep track of what and how much I actually eat. If I could remember what was in the empty plastic containers in the sink, I would know what I ate at my last meal (or last few meals, depending upon how long it's been since I emptied the sink). I've followed the toddler diet (cleaning off leftovers from my older son's plate), the stand-and-feed smorgasbord (standing in front of the refrigerator while eating, no temperature modification or utensils involved), and the double-dinner meal plan (eat with kids and then eat again with Daddy). The point is, I haven't really been paying attention.

Furthermore, I think my metabolism has slowed down as a result of quitting smoking, which surely contributed to my impressive fifty-pound first pregnancy weight gain that blossomed into a net gain of eighty pounds by the time I was ready to deliver the second time.

Of course, I know the formula for losing weight. Eat less and exercise more. Eating less would surely be easier if I slept more. Not only would I have fewer available hours in a day in which to eat, but I also wouldn't crave naughty foods because I was overtired. (I don't believe there's a magic way to reduce by eliminating whole food groups or combining food synergistically.)

I recently decided to make a conscious effort to watch what I eat and to make a point of exercising regularly every morning. As I've heard one of my exercise gurus say, "The longer a woman waits to exercise, the less likely she is to get around to it on any given day." That seems to be true in my experience.

I exercise at home, not because I don't want others to see me sweat, but because I can save time by not having to drive someplace, save laundry by not having to wear special clothes, and save even more time by not having to brush my teeth or perform other ablutions that usually precede leaving the house. I can even drink my morning coffee while working out, a practice that I am sure would be frowned upon in any gym. However, I do remember hearing that Arnold (Schwarzenegger) used to drink beer during his workouts; of course, that was back in the 1970s before we were enlightened. But the ultimate bottom-line key reason I exercise at home is . . . I don't need child care.

The fact that I don't have child care is precisely why I use videos at home—and why it sometimes takes more than the allotted time slot to complete a video (though still less than if I went someplace else).

My typical exercise routine goes something like this:

My younger son wakes up early—before it's even 5:30—after I have stayed up way too late working the night before. So I'm groggy, but figure that since only one of the kids is awake, especially this one, I might as well work out. My older son likes to decree, "No exercising, Mommy! No!" Then he will purposely try to trip me up or jump on me while I am doing the floor work.

So with him still snoozing, I put down the baby and pop in a tape of my current favorite guy (who does abs in every workout) and go to get a cup of coffee. But it's the previous night's old and yucky coffee, so I decide to make a fresh pot. That means I have to start the tape over. It's one of the routines I recorded myself from the Health Network on cable, and there is no introduction—it launches right into the warm-up.

I spend much of the routine trying to avoid the baby as he crawls around the room after me, wanting to practice pulling up. Another reason I exercise with this particular man these days is because he has really simple and straightforward routines (rather than dance numbers taught by very coordinated women who were probably world-class gymnasts or aerobics champions prior to hosting their own shows).

Midway through the first segment, Baby knocks my cup of coffee over onto our beige carpet. I know there is a break coming up—I've done this tape enough to know by heart the commercial I'd recorded along with the show—so I run to get paper towels and attack the mess. Fortunately, no coffee got on Baby (not that it was hot anymore, anyway), because that would have necessitated changing his clothes since he'd be going to day care that day. (It's one thing for me to go out of the house with coffee stains on my shirt, but what would people think if he did?)

Cleanup takes us through the commercial and beyond. I have to rewind the tape again.

Twice, I attempt to do the sit-up segment with my son lying across my chest for most of it. Halfway through the second time, my older son starts calling for me. I don't want Daddy to wake up, so I promptly stop the tape again and go to get my son.

"Mommy needs to finish exercising, okay?" I tell him.

"Okay, Mommy," he says.

I get him a cup of juice, which keeps him amused for most of the last segment of the tape before he starts antagonizing his brother. I stop the tape for the last time, doubtful that I'll resume it anytime that day, but I've just about made it to the end, so I'll call it done. I console myself with the thought that I can always do some leg lifts while I'm doing dishes or brushing my teeth.

My goal is to do this daily, even if it takes multiple attempts to get through one video and even if said attempts are not concurrent. I owe it to myself and to my children to live and model a healthy lifestyle.

Whoever said that having children changes everything was right. And for me, while most of the changes are welcome (once the initial shock wore off), the changes to my body are not. I love being a new mom. I just want my old body back!

Caroline B. Poser

This story has been adapted from the author's book MotherMorphosis, Vignettes about the Transformation Into and Within Motherhood, *Wyatt-MacKenzie Publishing, April 2006.*

That's What Friends Are For

The first sign that my expectations of motherhood were far from realistic came in my eighth month of pregnancy. After acing my Lamaze class and practically memorizing the chapters on labor and delivery in my pregnancy books, I awoke one night hemorrhaging. In all my years of dreaming about this night, I don't remember anything about bleeding all the way to the hospital while desperately trying to feel my daughter move.

Minutes after we reached the New Family Center (without the suitcase I'd had packed for weeks), the baby's heart stopped in vitro. Instead of my dream delivery, in which my husband, David, would hold my hand and offered encouragement while I panted like a dog, the midwife crooned, "Now push, honey," and a nurse dabbed sweat from my forehead, the delivery that ensued looked like a rerun of M*A*S*H.

Doctors and nurses collided into each other and knocked over trays of instruments. I caught one glimpse of David's face as a nurse pushed him from the room. My obstetrician staggered in half asleep but clearly panicked. For a split second, the anesthesiologist was above me saying something about, "Count to ten." Then nothing . . . until I awoke after a couple hours and was presented with a perfect little girl.

After I'd counted Haley's fingers and toes and cried over her little face, which that looked so much like her daddy's, my next thought was, *Well, so much for Lamaze.* Something told me this wasn't the last curve motherhood would throw me.

The next came the following day as I waddled down the hall of the maternity ward in search of a scale. An older woman passed, smiled, and offered, "Don't worry, sugar. You'll have that baby any minute now." She was gone before I could manage, "But I had her yesterday!" I found the scale and gingerly hoisted up one foot, then the other. My eyes fixed on the numbers in front of me; I inched the metal weights from left to right and stared in horror! Was this someone's idea of a joke? I'd delivered an eight-pound baby yesterday. Shouldn't I have lost at least eight pounds?

My third whammy came two nights later at home. Haley, who'd slept like an angel in the hospital, had been screaming her tiny head off since we'd brought her through the front door. Desperate for sleep, I raced to my library of crisp, new parenting books. Where was the chapter on how to get rid of colic? No such luck. The chapter I found, instead, was "Learning to Live with Colic." Why would I want to live with colic? It seemed a little like handing someone a travel brochure for Three Mile Island.

I spent the next four months pacing for hours at a time with a squalling infant in my arms, thinking, *I'm her mother. She's crying. I'm supposed to be able to make her stop. What's wrong with me? What's wrong with my baby? How could she scream all day and night and not grow up deranged?*

I tried everything, every trick I'd read about to get her back to sleep and a few I made up. I alternately ran the vacuum and the dryer. I bathed her in warm water. We walked in the backyard. I held her in all the positions illustrated in the books. I nursed and nursed and nursed. I even tried a suppository. Still she cried, and tired to my bones, I joined right in.

Things improved when Haley's schedule became at least more predictable. She continued to wake several times a night but was easier to get back to sleep. I got the shortest haircut I could stand to cut down my morning routine. Every little bit helped. Now that I could sleep enough to function, I had it all—everything I'd dreamed of during my pregnancy and during all those years when we were trying to get pregnant. So why wasn't I happy? Wasn't this the dream life I'd envisioned, a loving husband and a perfect baby? Okay, my social life was nonexistent, but I could work on that when sleep wasn't paramount.

My former coworkers were great, coming to visit, calling to check on me, and inviting Haley and me to lunch. But with David, the one person who loved Haley as much as I did, I felt isolated—even lonely. He offered to get up with her at night, but when she cried, he didn't stir. He just wasn't equipped with the same kind of receiver I had inside me that heard every breath Haley took. Not only that, but whatever he did for her wasn't the way I would have done it, and I had to resist the urge to redo it.

On the surface, I seemed like a happy and content little mama. Inside, though, I felt insecure, depressed, scared every minute I'd do something wrong, and lonely—oh, so lonely.

One day while looking at photo albums from my own childhood, I realized something. The photos of my mom and me included something that was missing from my life with Haley: other moms and their children. In the picture of me taking my first steps were the next-door neighbor and her twins. In the shot of me on the back patio happily wearing my lunch were the lady who lived down the block and her crew. Had the moms of the 1960s been on to something we hadn't figured out yet?

I thought about my own street: the elderly retired couple next door, the newlyweds on the other side, the grandparents across the street, and the people who seemed never to be home. Clearly, I wasn't going to find any comrades in my neighborhood. But the more I thought about those pictures of my mom and me, the more convinced I became that mom friends were the answer to all my woes.

I remembered reading in the local paper about a parenting center where moms and babies got together. I started asking around about it, and the next thing I knew, Haley and I were there. Walking through the doors, I couldn't remember ever feeling that shy and unsure of myself. I felt like an imposter. These other women knew what they were doing. They were real moms. They'd take one look at me and see how inadequate I was at this mommy thing.

But then an amazing thing happened. We started talking—about our deliveries, our recoveries, our sleepless nights, our breastfeeding difficulties—and the more we talked, the better I felt. Like someone dying of thirst who's given a canteen of water, I couldn't get enough. Where I'd rationed myself at the office to talk only so long about Haley's reflux problem or the amazing way she'd started lifting herself up on her arms, here in the company of these moms, I could let it rip. I could talk about poop, runny noses, diaper rash on her little butt, anything I wanted, and it was received with enthusiasm and, even more important, complete understanding.

To my surprise, these women felt the same doubt, the same guilt, and the same worries, which until then had seemed to be mine alone. I found myself laughing about the very things that had me crying the night before. We laughed about finally getting the baby to sleep, only to jump up and check her breathing every two minutes, about falling asleep while someone was talking to us, about gladly choosing sleep over sex, about putting a drop of baby shampoo in our own eye to make sure it was really tear-free. I wasn't alone anymore. When I showed them how I'd only manicured one hand before Haley started crying and had never gotten back to the other, another mom rolled up her pants legs and showed how she'd shaved only one leg. We laughed until we cried. I felt drunk!

At times, we all talked at once. We even took to having paper nearby to jot down what we wanted to say when we finally got a chance to speak. When the center closed, we hung around the parking lot talking, not ready to let each other go. As much as Haley depended on me for the things she needed, I began to depend on my mom–friends for reassurance and encouragement, for sanity. Each time I visited with my mom friends, I came home a more content and competent mom, a happier wife, a more productive employee, and a better person.

It's been thirteen years and two more kids since my first visit to the parenting center. Some of the moms I've met there have come and gone from my life. But some of us have become family. We've seen each other through death, divorce, unemployment, pregnancy, the birth of more than a dozen babies, and myriad stages of childhood. We've laughed together, cried together, swapped parenting tips and baby-sitting, shared maternity and baby clothes, and buoyed each other again and again. Looking back on that lonely, incompetent mom I was thirteen years ago, I wonder if I could have done it without my mom–friends. I know I couldn't have done it as well. And it looks like I'll be needing their support as much as ever now that number four is on his way.

Mimi Greenwood Knight

This story was first published in Christian Parenting Today, *Summer 2005.*

Finding My Comfort Zone

By the time the baby arrived, I considered myself a walking encyclopedia on infant care. Still a college undergrad, I'd approached impending motherhood with the same zeal I'd put into cramming for finals. I'd committed to memory the advice of Spock and other childrearing experts. I'd quizzed friends who had already given birth. I'd even managed to coax tips from my evasive obstetrician, who seemed to show little interest in babies once they arrived.

If there'd been a Trivial Pursuit or Jeopardy category on neonates, I'd have nailed it. I intended to get an A-plus in the parenting game. Allergies, cradle cap, diaper rash, burping, colic—I'd studied it all. I felt one hundred percent prepared for motherhood.

When we brought sound-asleep Steve home from the hospital that chilly February afternoon, I installed him in his bassinet. I layered him with a pair of aqua receiving blankets, settled myself in my bird's-eye maple rocker, and then glanced around at the Little Bo Peep and Hey Diddle Diddle plywood cutouts I'd tacked to the creamy-lemon nursery walls. Everything looked perfect. Until then, though, readying the room for the baby had somehow seemed like fixing up a doll house. Now, I looked down at Steve, and he emitted a nearly inaudible snore. No doll did that. *So this is paradise,* I told myself, *pure bliss.*

When my hovering husband suggested that Steve's perfect upbringing could be put on hold while we took a lunch break, I hungrily agreed.

"How does chicken soup sound?"

"It sounds heavenly," I answered. "I'll eat it right here in the nursery where I can keep an eye on our baby."

We exchanged conspiratorial smiles. I wondered how long we'd be playing at parenthood before we truly felt comfortable in our new roles.

As Bob carried my tray into the room, Steve awakened with a yowl. By the time I got him changed and fed, my soup had grown cold. Glumly, I spooned it down, not wanting to bother Bob about reheating it. Trouble had entered paradise.

I'd never dreamed that the tower of tidily folded diapers on Steve's bureau could dwindle so quickly or that I'd weary so soon of feeding on demand. By twilight,

I'd alternately nursed and changed so many times that I broke into exhausted sobs. "I'm so worn out," I wailed.

"Let me call my mother," Bob offered. "You need some rest, and she'd be tickled to be here."

My elderly German mother-in-law had retired a few years earlier from a lifelong career in nursing. When it came to babies, she represented intimidating authority. I was apprehensive, but Bob looked so eager. Wanting to please, I reluctantly agreed. Besides, it would be a welcome relief to get some rest.

Nana arrived shortly and took over changing chores while I bathed and took a nap. When I awoke, my cotton nightie clung clammily to my chest. Checking Steve, I found his tiny forehead beaded with sweat. Nana had hiked up the thermostat about ten degrees. The entire house felt like a sauna. But I didn't want to say anything to hurt her feelings, so I crawled back into bed.

I awoke the next morning, a Sunday, to the scent of cinnamon wafting from the kitchen. I figured Nana was baking her signature apple strudel. I'd hinted the night before that I needed to start shedding some of the pounds I'd gained during pregnancy, but she'd just laughed when I asked if she could prepare some dietetic gelatin.

"You'll lose plenty of weight just nursing," she'd said.

Deciding the diet could wait a week or two, I devoured all the oatmeal and applesauce and ended up accepting seconds on the strudel. The nourishment provided me with enough strength to approach Nana about the heat.

"Don't you think it's a little warm in here?" I asked.

"It's winter, dear. You need to keep the house warm for the baby."

I sighed. Maybe she really knew best. After all, she'd been a registered nurse.

As the week progressed, so did my sense of frustration. While I'd read that nursing mothers should abstain from alcohol, Nana claimed beer was good for producing milk and served me a stein with lunch. She looked miffed when I declined to drink it. When I offered to let visiting neighbors hold Steve, Nana claimed that he shouldn't be exposed to their germs. She scowled when I handed over the baby anyway.

Despite the stifling house, Nana insisted on swaddling the baby, swearing that being tightly wrapped would comfort him, make him feel secure. Nana might have thought Steve felt secure; I sure didn't. With a knot in my stomach, I watched as Steve's little face knotted while his whole body struggled against the confines of the heavy blanket.

On Saturday morning, when I'd been home from the hospital a week, I decided to tidy the house. Nana had put most of her energy into cooking and into changing and bathing Steve. However, some of the routine chores I'd always taken care of had been neglected. Polishing up the place would lift my spirits. I wandered from room to room, taking inventory. The vacuuming and dusting could wait another day or two, but the kitchen floor was littered with crumbs. I grabbed the broom, thinking I'd sweep first and then tackle the dishes heaped in the sink.

Nana came wheeling into the house from the backyard, where she had been hanging out bed sheets. Wresting the broom from my hands, she growled, "You shouldn't be doing that. It's too soon for any exercise. Get back in bed!"

"I just wa-wa-wanted to sweep up a little," I stammered.

"You heard me. Now get back in bed. I can do this later." She shook her head and leaned the broom against the refrigerator. "Off you go!"

Stunned, I shuffled back to bed like an obedient four-year-old.

But I stewed and simmered. It was our house, I reasoned. It was my life. And though just out of my teens, I was not a child. I was supposed to be a mother.

In the late afternoon, I finally made a decision. I approached Bob. "Look," I began timidly, "I've tried to please everybody—you, your mother, the baby, friends, Dr. Spock, even the obstetrician. But it's just not working. There's room here for only one mother, and it has to be me."

"Great," he said, breaking into a relieved grin. "Mom's anxious to get home. And I'm ready for some privacy, too."

I just stared at him. In my anxiety to please, I'd overlooked the effects of my passive conduct. By not speaking up, ignoring my own comfort quotient, and behaving like a good little girl and an acquiescent student, I'd permitted discomfort to flourish all around.

I also had been slow to recognize that parenting differed from taking a class at school. Though we could seek out expertise, Bob and I would have to arrive at answers together. There'd be nobody to critique us, nobody to tell us if we'd passed or failed. We'd have to choose the course of action that made us feel comfortable.

"I appreciate all that your mother's done. I am so grateful, and we'll thank her together," I said, reaching over to loosen Steve's swaddling blanket. "But now I'm in charge."

Bob looked relieved. Steve sighed, flailing his unfettered feet. Suddenly, I felt quite grown up and motherly. Perhaps paradise had been regained.

Terri Elders

Welcome Home

"So they're going to let us take her home now?" I can still remember the look on his face and the angst in his voice when my husband asked me this question. We had just signed a pile of discharge papers and were preparing to leave the shelter of the maternity wing, where we had been guided through everything from breastfeeding to diaper changes.

"I guess so," I answered him with a nervous smile, as I gingerly placed the baby in her infant carrier and adjusted the straps to fit snugly around her. She looked so tiny in the giant car seat.

By hospital standards, we were ready to venture out into the cosmic world of parenthood on our own. We anxiously waited for an orderly to come in with a wheelchair and courteously push me out to the car, but after several minutes, there was still no one in sight. I finally assumed the wheelchair scenario was only something you see in the movies. Instead, my husband and I walked along the empty hallway and through the labor-and-delivery doors, infant seat securely in hand. Both excitement and apprehension followed us down the elevator and into the parking lot. I eased myself into the back seat as my husband carefully snapped our baby's carrier into its silver base. Then he proceeded to drive at least ten miles under the speed limit the entire way home. It's safe to say as brand-new parents, we were feeling a bit underqualified to take on the huge responsibility buckled in next to me.

That may seem kind of odd coming from a twenty-seven-year-old woman who was a fourth-grade teacher responsible for twenty-two children six hours a day, five days a week.

The school year had just begun when those faint blue lines finally made their appearance in the pregnancy test's window. My husband and I had been trying to conceive for almost a year, though the baby bug had bitten me long before. As much as I loved teaching, my heart ached to be a mother. Diaper commercials made me weepy. I couldn't even watch those reality baby stories on television without a box of tissue. At my last check-up, my doctor had suggested that we consider fertility testing. I was devastated to even think about the possibility that we could not conceive.

Before setting up our first consultation with a fertility specialist, I decided to take another pregnancy test. Those two minutes seemed like an eternity as fretful questions plagued my mind. *What if it's negative again? Will I need to make that appointment? Is something wrong with me? Oh, please let it be positive* . . . And it was! My husband and I could hardly believe our eyes as we looked at that life-changing plastic stick. In disbelief, I took three more tests during the next twenty-four hours just to be sure. Positive! Positive! Positive!

Within the week, I bought a slew of pregnancy books, registered for the prenatal classes, and started the hunt for reasonably priced baby furniture. By the time I was barely seven months along, my hospital bag was packed, the baby's room was decorated, and her dresser drawers were filled to the brim with pastel-colored onesies, socks, rompers, and sleeping gowns. Almost every day I would sit on the glider in the nursery admiring the classic Pooh Bear décor and the fluffy clouds I had sponged ever so carefully on the sky-blue walls. My hands rested on my growing belly as I envisioned holding our sweet baby in my arms. I imagined how peaceful she would look sleeping in her crib and how her eyes would light up when she noticed the animals on her mobile for the first time. I had already fallen in love with this baby, and I hadn't even met her yet.

Six baby showers, dozens of Oreos, and count-less late-night bathroom trips later, the big day finally arrived. I had never expected to schedule an appoint-ment to have my baby, but after a week of doctor-prescribed bed rest and drinking so much water I thought I'd drown, my amniotic fluid level still wasn't up to par. My doctor advised that we go ahead and deliver the baby nine days early. Although I couldn't wait to see her ten tiny fingers and ten tiny toes, the thought of being induced was somewhat bittersweet. Pitocin just isn't the friendliest sounding word. Naive as it sounds, I had always pictured the typical sitcom scenario: waking up in the middle of the night, squint-ing in pain from a whopper contraction, shaking my snoring husband, and yelling, "Honey, it's time!" He'd jump out of bed, run frantically in circles, grab the keys and my suitcase, hop in the car, and start backing out of the driveway before realizing that I was still waddling down the front steps trying to catch up with him.

Instead, we arrived at the hospital at exactly the scheduled time, 3:00 P.M., and got right down to busi-ness. My actual induction was set for six o'clock the next morning, but the prep work began that after-noon. A labor-and-delivery nurse escorted me to a birthing room with my husband following behind, up to his eyeballs in suitcases, pillows, a video cam-era, snacks, bottled water, you name it. It must have looked like we were moving in. I caught a glimpse of the nurses smiling at our Boy Scout–like preparedness. We might as well have had "First-Time Parents" tattooed on our foreheads.

We had hardly walked through the door, when another nurse handed me a blue-and-white checkered hospital gown and said I could change in the bathroom. Nodding, I took the gown from her, walked into the bathroom, and closed the door. I slid my arms through the gaping holes of the gown and attempted to tie the strings around my snowman-like figure.

That's when it hit me. As scenes from those agonizing natural childbirth videos flashed before my eyes, my heart began to pound and my mind began to race. *I can't do this. I'm scared. What if something goes wrong? I really don't think I can do this. Can't I just skip this part and have my baby magically appear?*

Then, almost as quickly, those anxious thoughts were washed away by the encouraging words I'd received from moms who had bravely gone before. "You'll be fine." "Women have babies every day." "They'll take good care of you." "Are you getting an epidural? Good; they don't hand out any medals for going natural." An unexpected laugh escaped my lips as I looked down at my protruding belly and thought to myself, *There's no going back now even if I wanted to. I can do this.*

Taking a deep breath, I lifted the handle on the bathroom door. As I slowly walked over to the hospital bed, I noticed the baby bassinet in the corner of the room lined with pink-and-teal-striped receiving blankets. The warming lamp perched above seemed to anticipate my baby's arrival. I glanced at the empty bassinet countless times during the next several hours, knowing that sometime tomorrow a new little person would be lying there. With that image in my mind, I drifted off to sleep, looking forward to my 6:00 A.M. wake-up call.

Shortly after two o'clock, I woke suddenly, squinting in pain. Surprisingly, I had gone into labor on my own, Pitocin-free! But instead of shaking my snoring husband, I pressed the call button and politely said, "I think my water just broke." At the sound of my voice, the half-asleep daddy-to-be jumped up and proceeded to run around in circles, making sure I had ice chips, cold washcloths, and that the anesthesiologist was on his way. Most essentially, he let me squeeze his hand so hard his fingers almost popped off, and he didn't even grimace.

Three different nurses, two epidurals, and one last "Give it all you've got!" push later, and our baby girl did, indeed, magically appear. The moment I heard her cry, my eyes spilled over with tears. Feelings of gratitude, strength, relief, and empowerment overwhelmed me. I knew I had done something great. I knew I had been given something great. My husband was still holding my hand as I looked up into his misty eyes. They seemed to sparkle with amazement as he gazed at our daughter. This beautiful baby we had longed for was now entrusted to us, her mother and father, to love, teach, nurture, guide, and protect.

As the nurse laid my daughter's warm, squishy body against my chest, I fell in love with her all over again. She fit so perfectly in my arms, as if she were always meant to be there. Holding her felt so natural, yet it was so surreal to look into her dark blue eyes and know that she was mine.

Even on the deliberately slow drive home, I was still in awe of our little creation snoozing away in her car seat.

We pulled up to our house to find the front lawn sporting a new "Welcome" sign for our baby girl, specially made by her new grandpa. As we opened our front door, the crisp smell of Pine-Sol and the hum of the dishwasher greeted us. Vacuum lines adorned the carpet. The bathtubs sparkled, and our refrigerator glistened inside and out. It felt like an episode of *Extreme Home Makeover*, courtesy of my mom.

Never before had our house felt more like a home. This was where our daughter would learn and grow, where we would see her smile and hear her coo for the first time. Down the hallway, she would take her first steps while her daddy and I cheered her on. In the kitchen, she would be covered in frosting after demolishing her first birthday cake. Out in the backyard, the grass would tickle her bare feet as she toddled after a butterfly. Under this roof, my husband and I would learn and grow right along with her as we embraced our new roles as parents. This was the home where we would become a family.

My daughter's wrinkled feet peeked out from underneath her Pooh Bear blanket tucked around her fidgety legs. She curled her hands into small fists and started to cry. Glancing at the clock, I realized it had been almost two hours since she had eaten. I scooped up my baby girl and carried her into the nursery. I sat down on the glider and gently shushed her while she nursed and we rocked back and forth, just as I had imagined so many times before. As she nuzzled close to me, a sense of peace seemed to quiet my insecurities about being a new mom. *Yes, I can do this.*

I put my daughter's hand in mine, kissed her tiny fingers, and whispered, "I love you, sweetheart. I'm so glad you're home."

Kelli Perkins

Froggy Feet

Oh my! What tiny feet. I cradled the soft heel of Ben's right foot in my palm and traced my huge finger along the curve of his toes. One, two, three, four, five toes.

But wait! Two of the toes in the middle were stuck together. And the left foot had the same issue. What was this?

For the first time in the postpartum unit, I pushed the nurse call light. I was almost afraid to touch the webbed toes, as if the abnormality might be a source of pain for my newborn son, Benjamin. But as he suckled away on his bottle, I cautiously traced the line of joined skin. He did not flinch or jerk away.

A kind-faced nurse bustled in. "Can I help you, dear?" she asked.

I didn't know what to say. Here was my perfect new baby and I had just found a defect, something unexpected and confounding. Words wouldn't form properly in my mind, so I extended his leg a little closer to her face.

"Yes," she said. "I see those little feet. Want to play *Piggy Goes to Market*? Oh, I see. Yes, webbed toes."

"Webbed toes!" I sputtered out. "Why didn't anyone notice before? It's been almost a whole day. Are they okay? Does it hurt him? Will he walk normally?"

"Nothing to worry about," she said, patting my arm. "I've seen it a few times. Shouldn't mean a thing."

Shouldn't or wouldn't? Big difference there.

She got called away, so I couldn't ask her who she had seen it on before or what caused it. I phoned my husband, Dan, and told him about it. I was utterly disappointed in the parents, grandparents, aunts, and uncles who had held Ben all day long, not to mention the nurses and doctors who delivered him. Why hadn't anyone noticed?

Dan assured me we would talk to the doctors tomorrow. He handed over the phone to my three-year-old daughter, Maggie. Distractedly, I sang her our homemade Goodnight Song.

"Get some rest," Dan said. "I am sure Ben is fine."

At first, rest eluded me, though Ben managed to nap in the bassinet. Periodically, I would roll onto my side, get up, and peek inside his blanket to inspect his elbow or his ear. Could we have overlooked something else odd?

Earlier in the day I had admired Ben's delicate features with total new-mom amazement and joy. First, I soaked in his gorgeous, big eyes, so wise and knowing despite his newness, covered in thick lashes any woman would die for. Lips like cupid's bow. Nose as cute as a button. Tufts of dark brown hair covering his head, just like his daddy. Oh, what a lady killer he would be. I, for one, was already prepared to forgive any misdeed on his part. Juice stains on carpets, baseballs through windows, or even wrecking my car would be pardoned with his simple charm.

I was deep in mommy love.

Even more amazing was that I had already marveled over these very things three years ago when Maggie was born. I assumed my second pregnancy would hold little suspense beyond discovery of a new personality. I knew without a doubt that child number two would emerge fully formed and developed. Each part would be in full working order. No user manual needed. I was a seasoned pro.

Was I ever wrong! Everything about Ben surprised me. Sure, both children shared similar coloring and size, but his nose was broader and his eyes held a clever, different expression from her curious one. Here was an entirely new and unique person to meet.

And now the toes.

Finally, after feedings, diaper changes, and little sleep, the morning arrived with return visitors. Everyone had an opinion about this development. One grandmother declared he would forever be made fun of in the locker rooms. Another grandmother said that God made him just the way he was supposed to be. Dan came in with some Internet printouts that provided prognoses ranging from webbed toes being a benign condition to them being associated with extremely rare and scary diseases.

Although we were concerned, simple pleasures kept most of the worry away. The enigma of Ben's feet hid behind the comfort of Maggie's hugs and the joy of getting acquainted with Ben.

Finally, the pediatrician arrived. We unwrapped Ben's feet, and the doctor quickly examined the toes and conducted the routine one-day-old checkup.

"What do webbed toes mean?" I asked. "Will he walk? Does it hurt him?"

He assured me the issue was purely cosmetic. "It may even help him swim faster," he said with a wry smile. "We'll talk about options at the six-week visit."

Later that day we drove home with our balloons, flowers, and new baby. Maggie, the proud sister, immediately paraded stuffed animals for Ben's entertainment. A warm feeling of contentment tried to enter my heart, swelled by the completeness of our family. If only the questions cluttering my mind would stop my thoughts from returning to those little webbed toes.

On one particularly long and trying night, Ben and I sprawled out together on a comforter in the living room. Having soaked through two outfits already, Ben lay wrapped in a blanket, while I tried to remember if I had finished drying his other sleepers earlier that day.

With a jerk of his arm, he flung off the blanket and brushed my upper arm as if to say, *Get a move on it, Mom.* I rolled to my side and looked into his eyes.

How lucky I am to be his mother, I thought, and smiled.

As I located his clothes, I decided right then and there to stop obsessing over his condition. There was nothing to be done about it right now, anyway, so why not just enjoy him?

I spent the remainder of my first six postpartum weeks doing just that. Sure, an occasional negative thought would invade when my defenses were down. Bouts of colic turned my thoughts to rare syndromes and mounting medical issues. I would swipe away the unhelpful notions, knowing that any screaming baby would panic a mother into desperate explanations.

Dan joined me for the six-week appointment with the pediatrician. The doctor immediately reviewed Ben's clinical findings, all normal. Sufficient weight gain. Good rooting and sucking reflexes. No signs of distress.

Finally, he turned to options for the webbed toes. Considering the cosmetic basis of the condition, we had two alternatives. *Only two*, I couldn't help thinking. One was surgery. The other was to leave it be.

The doctor stood and handed my husband a surgeon's referral card. "The choice is completely up to you," he said. "But you want to wait until he's at least one year old for a procedure. No need for undue trauma this early."

Trauma, indeed. Thoughts of needles, scalpels, and bandages haunted me. Researching general anesthesia, with its risks of adverse reactions and respiratory problems, provided more horror. No way, I decided. I could not put my one-year-old baby boy through surgery for something superficial. Ben could avoid sandals if he had psychological issues with it.

Dan, on the other hand, saw little to stop a surgical procedure. Minor surgery, he said. Just two quick slices, a few bandages, and forever normal feet.

Seeing as there was no pressure for an immediate decision, we held off any sort of compromise.

Then one warm spring day brought a resolution. After being cooped up inside all winter, the whole family was enjoying the newly green trees under the bright sunshine. We played catch and then settled down on a picnic blanket for a rest. Maggie kicked off her shoes, and we all followed suit.

"Froggy feet," Maggie said and yanked on Ben's big toe. "He's got feet like frogs, all connected in the middle."

Across the blanket, my eyes met Dan's.

"How do you know that?" I asked.

"Kermit," she said and rolled toward her dad.

I laughed and lay back with my hands behind my head. The Muppet character, Kermit the Frog, possessed flat, uninteresting feet. Maggie enjoyed watching and reading about Kermit. I'd turned that interest into a mini biology lesson a few months before. Looking at pictures of real frogs and tadpoles had provided a link to Kermit's inspiration and, apparently, a lasting impression of their unique toes.

"Oh," I said. "They are froggy feet. And they are just perfect the way they are."

I leaned down to place a kiss on each foot.

Dan squinted through the sunshine and nodded his head.

"Are you saying that to avoid surgery?" he asked.

"No," I said. "I love Ben just as he is."

So, with that, Dan relented to our noninvasive plan. If Ben disliked his feet's appearance when he was old enough to decide, he could undergo a procedure in the future. For now, the froggy feet were here to stay.

After two years, Ben walks upright with no hint of a ribbit or an affinity for flies. And I am still blissfully proud of both my children, just as they are.

Jodi Gastaldo

Small Sacrifices

What follows is a tale of my self-diagnosis and home treatment of a suspected case of post-partum depression. Please, do not try this at home.

July 2006

It's been eighteen months of trying to get pregnant, and we have an appointment to see a specialist in ten days. I'm dreading the idea of the needles, stress, and expense again; we've traveled this road before, to conceive our three-year-old son.

When my period is one day late, I decide to take a home pregnancy test so I won't freak out over possibly being pregnant when I know I'm not. If the result is negative, which I expect it to be, I intend to just get over it.

My jaw swings open to my chest when I see the second line appear.

My husband says, "Don't we have to wait three minutes?"

I explain that the line won't fade away once it appears. In shock, I utter an expletive along the lines of "sacred excrement."

November 2006
We clearly see girl parts on the ultrasound, and all her other parts look healthy. We'll have a complete set, a boy and a girl. What could be more perfect?

Late March 2007
The baby is more than a week late. I routinely sob in her finished lavender nursery with the stenciled dragonflies, butterflies, and flowers in coordinating purple. I stare at her baby clothes and weep with exhaustion and discomfort. This enormous baby has her feet in my ribcage, and I am comfortable only when sitting ramrod straight or lying on my side, which I rarely get to do now that my son has given up naps. I pray fervently for labor every quiet moment and curse God when my contractions come to nothing. This lack of perspective foreshadows the coming months.

Easter Sunday 2007

At four days old, Avery Lynn is gorgeous, perfect, and huge at nine and a half pounds. People marvel at how she came out of my formerly petite body, but my ravaged pelvic floor knows exactly how. Sitting is a frightening and tentative exercise.

My milk comes in this very day, and the only shirt that fits over my stripper-size boobs is my husband's. I feel like a lactating whale. These huge breasts are also as hard as billiard balls. The slightest touch sends radiating darts of pain across their stretched surface.

Spring 2007

I wonder how I ever thought one single child was hard. Now that I have two, one or the other, or both, needs something every moment, and if they don't, there's a dish that needs washing, a floor that needs sweeping, or a shower that needs taking. I'm also racked with guilt that I'm ignoring my precious First Born, so I push cars along the floor with him. Then I'm racked with guilt that I'm ignoring my Baby Girl, who is content to swing or to watch us from her bouncy seat. So I pick her up, even though I don't really need to. And put her down to play more cars. And to make lunch. And to get crumbs in her hair by eating a sandwich while nursing at the kitchen table so I can share lunchtime with First Born.

At first, nursing is agony. My left side is so painful that latching her on is like slamming my breast in a car door. I get her all lined up to nurse, and lose my nerve. Eventually, Lansinoh saves my poor cracked nipple. I remain ambivalent about nursing. I want to swill caffeine all day to keep myself awake, eat junk if I feel inclined to do so, and have a glass of wine—maybe two if I'm feeling really wild—in a quiet moment at night. I do let myself have a glass of wine now and then (even La Leche League says it's okay), but I plot and plan how to accomplish it and then feel racked with guilt. Again, here comes the racking guilt, always the racking guilt . . . because a good mother would give it all up, just to be sure. And she wouldn't mind, either. Small sacrifice, right? I mean, how petty and shallow can I be? I'm a forgiving person to everyone but myself. For my own performance, I'm harsher than Simon Cowell crossed with Supernanny and Judge Judy.

I complain to a friend, who reminds me of how very, very blessed I am. I hate myself for complaining in the face of such blessing.

June 2007

I'm walking with a friend at an outdoor event. I catch a glimpse of myself in the side of a shiny glass building and I flinch away. I would like to throw myself on the concrete and sob. In a vain effort to wear normal clothes instead of maternity wear, my soft belly juts out in front of me. I look distinctly three months pregnant. Everyone I see around me floats by in gauzy, diaphanous summer dresses or in cute, clingy tops and shorts. I hate myself for this vanity. But it's a sacrifice, isn't it, for such a precious miracle?

We've put a mirror above the baby's changing table so I can hold her up to it in her sweet little outfits. But as I change diapers, I look up to see a hag with ratty hair, a puffy face, and dark circles so heavy it's like someone punched me in the nose. I hate my ugly self, and I hate myself for caring. Small sacrifice, right?

I Google postpartum depression and decide I don't have it. Well, probably not. I mean, I don't think so. I am still able to get out of bed. I don't feel like harming the kids or myself. I still feel connected to my children. I still love them very much.

Mostly, it's anxiety, I decide. I torture myself with waking nightmares of a kidnapper stealing one of my kids while I'm distracted by the other—because, obviously, having two kids is too much for me. As I set my baby in her seat on the garage floor to get my son in the car, a horror-show vision of the garage door coming down to crush her flashes into my brain. She's several feet from the garage door, and why would it randomly come down, anyway? I can't shake that image, though, and think of it every time we all get in the car.

Not all is bleak. My son is funny and sweet and adores his sister. He's a big help in little ways, like bringing me diapers and entertaining himself while I nurse. He holds up his shirt and pretends to nurse a doll, which is beyond hilarious. Walks around the block on pretty days are like salve to my anxious soul. One particular sunny day, the baby and I lounge in the shade, and my son plays in his wading pool. Weekend family outings are fun, because I have backup in the form of my husband. Then Monday returns, something goes wrong, and the anxiety rears up once again.

August 2007
The bottle strike begins. My oasis of sanity is to let my Baby Girl have a bottle of breastmilk or formula once in a while. But at four months old, she will have none of it. I can see nothing ahead of me but thousands of breastfeedings at all hours of day and night.

My husband says he's worried about me because my sense of humor is gone. I read his concern as criticism and attack him for expecting so much out of me at a time like this. He does the only thing he can think of: he insists I leave the house on Tuesday evenings the minute he gets home. I go to coffee shops and write. I look forward to those days like an addict needing a hit.

September 2007

I wean from the breast. Guilt-racking begins in earnest, but I decide that the ambivalence I feel, right or wrong, is hurting my relationship with the baby. It's certainly hurting me. I'm relieved, maybe slightly torn, when I nurse for the last time, cuddled up in bed.

As if to taunt me for my selfish decision, my breasts continue to leak for weeks on end. Then, the minute I wean, it's discovered that my baby is allergic to several foods, including both cow's milk and soy. Now, she can only consume a formula nearly as expensive as gold dust.

Our second car dies. I'm not working. Financial panic now sets in, on top of the guilt, because if I were still nursing . . .

My Tuesday writing sessions can't come often enough, and on those nights when my husband is a smidge late from work, cutting into my golden ninety minutes, I can feel my hands itching. *Must get out. Need this time. Can't he drive eighty-five? Everyone else does.*

Then, I take a voice class. I sign up just before the car dies, and it's nonrefundable, so I go anyway, though we shouldn't have spent the money. At voice class, I meet fun people, including our funny and sweet instructor, Amy. I learn how to sing properly. My voice reaches notes I didn't know were possible. I figure out how to project my voice "forward," and the music rings out clear and strong, no more mousy, breathy sound. My assigned song is perky and cute, suitable for someone much younger, and I feel younger. I've gotten slimmer, too. My classmates exclaim they can't believe I gave birth to such a huge baby only six months before. And I'm pleased. I don't care if it's shallow, because it feels good. It feels good when Amy praises my singing, my progress. It feels like coming home after a long voyage to strange lands, because this is how I normally am: positive, happy, appreciative of my husband's weird humor.

I don't know to this day (as I write this, my baby is about to turn one year old) if I really had postpartum depression. What does it really matter? Why do we have to be clinically diagnosed to take care of ourselves, to acknowledge that all is not normal? Why should we wait until total system meltdown to ask for a helping hand? It's that insidious sickly guilt that stops us. Even now, my inner Simon Cowell/ Judge Judy/Supernanny wants me to hit the delete key, saying, *Oh, stop! You're just being dramatic. So it was rough. Suck it up, buttercup.*

I meant what I said about not trying this at home. I let shame stop me from saying to my husband, to my family, to my friends, "I'm exhausted. I need more sleep. I'm not as happy as I pretend to be. I'm having a hard time. I can't cook dinner all the time. I have to let the dishes pile up, and you have to reassure me it's okay, because I hate myself for failing and I feel like I'm failing all the time." Because even just speaking the words out loud might have robbed my anxiety of its power, might have rushed me along to contentment. And what if it all had gone downhill? Maybe one more disaster would have propelled me into classic "warning sign" territory. The consequences of that are too frightening to ponder.

But that did not happen. My Tuesday night writing binges and my voice class and when precious Avery finally slept through the night in December (Merry Christmas, Mommy!), and the wacky humor of my five-year-old boy and the concern of my sweet husband all helped me to let up on myself. In the end, my trials proved to be small sacrifices, after all.

Kristina Riggle

Battle of the Breast

"He's still not doing it," I said, my voice barely above a whisper. I couldn't look at my husband, hovering over me in the pediatrician's office, hopeful. "It feels no different."

The nurse, Connie, a woman in her fifties who'd already told me she had an adult daughter going through the same thing, came over and put her arms around me. My head dropped to her hip. "It's all right, honey," she said. "We'll get this working." I started to cry for the second time that hour. "It'll be okay," she assured me. But I wasn't so sure.

Eleven days earlier, Aidan had been born with a tongue-tie. The fleshy, stringy part beneath his tongue prevented him from extending his tongue past his lips. Everyone—my husband, the pediatrician, the nurses, and I—thought that after the five-minute surgery he'd had Aidan would be able to breastfeed. But it didn't happen. So far, clipping his tongue wasn't the miracle cure we were hoping for.

"It'll take time," Connie said, sighing. "He's not used to it yet. He had that tied tongue for nine months inside you."

Breastfeeding was proving to be the most difficult thing I'd ever done. I'd never imagined it would be so difficult . . . or painful. But my little boy just couldn't get the hang of it.

Aidan's third week of life consisted of continuous attempts to breastfeed along with "finger feedings" to make sure he was getting enough nourishment. I would thread one end of a tiny tube through the nipple of a baby bottle and attach the other to my forefinger with tape. Then I'd insert my finger into Aidan's mouth, and he would suck the pumped breastmilk through the tube and up into his mouth. When he did this, I knew that sucking wasn't his problem. By the end of week three, however, having only finger-fed him at night, I believed that we'd improved on the breast, even if it wasn't perfect.

Laura, a tall, slender nurse who looked fresh out of nursing school, visited my home often after Aidan's tongue clipping. At the end of his third week, it was time to weigh him.

"You ready?" she asked, standing over me in my living room. With my baby in my arms, I sat, nervous, on the edge of my couch. Laura bent down, her long, blond hair spilling out of a knot, and ran a smooth finger across Aidan's cheek. "He looks great." He stirred, opening his eyes.

"He's nursed nonstop," I said. Even though it hurt to nurse and Aidan still hadn't extended his tongue past his lips, I was certain that, with all the time he'd lain cradled at my breast, he had to have quadrupled his weight . . . or at least gained a few ounces.

Laura pulled her portable infant scale out of the canvas bag she'd brought with her and set in on the floor. I peeled open Aidan's tiny diaper with trembling hands and placed him, naked, on the cold, metal scale. As the scale calibrated Aidan's weight, I bit my lip, waiting.

Laura and I leaned forward to see the verdict. At once, both our faces fell.

"Oh," she said. "He's down four ounces."

I scrunched up my face, examining the numbers, confused. "I thought for sure he was getting enough milk," I said. I wanted to sound pulled together, but my voice shook and fat, fresh tears gave me away. Like a shell washed onto the shore, I sat there, vulnerable and stuck.

It turned out that Aidan had never latched on correctly. I soon realized I didn't know what a good latch felt like. In my journal, I had written, "Aidan will suckle for forty-five minutes and still be ravenous." Apparently, I was doing something very wrong.

Over the next couple weeks, public health nurses came and went, checking on our progress at the breast and weighing Aidan. Not only was Aidan not latching on correctly, he would also clamp down with his jaw and grind away on my nipple with his gums. Aside from his birth, I had never experienced such excruciating pain. My toes curled on the carpet when he tried to nurse. Yet, I thought that the pain was normal, that Aidan was actually nursing.

Perhaps things would have been different had Aidan been born in a different place and at a different time. As it were, my son was born the evening of July 3, 2007, in Fairbanks, a town of about 80,000 people, in central Alaska. Likely due to the national holiday the following day, nurses with any lactation know-how had the day off.

Aidan arrived at 7:36 P.M., pink and startled. Uninterested in my clumsy attempts to cajole him into sucking for milk, he drank nothing that night or the following morning. Not until late in the afternoon on the following day did Aidan finally get food into his stomach. But he'd already lost weight. And I'd begun to panic.

A woman who looked more like a prison guard than a hospital nurse introduced tiny bottles of formula and taught me how to finger-feed. "I've never done this before," she said, threading the tube through the bottle. "But I think this is how it goes."

I left the hospital two days after Aidan's birth, a little uneasy. With my newborn tucked into his car seat and my husband at my side, I hobbled out of my hospital room, my cocoon of safety, feeling anxious but with no idea of how difficult the road ahead would be.

Before giving birth, I'd thought breastfeeding might feel weird, embarrassing even, like being caught in the supermarket with my skirt tucked into my tights. I never seriously considered that I might encounter obstacles that would interfere with my ability to breast-feed. As it turned out, those obstacles made me even more determined to nurse my newborn son.

Once my milk came in, my breasts, engorged and sore, dripped nonstop, like leaky faucets. Milk stained our platform bed, the kitchen floor, the couch, the table. Everywhere I went, I left a trail. The smell of sour milk permeated the air. Aidan's futile and frantic attempts to nurse soon left my nipples cracked, blistered, and bright red. I'd read somewhere that I shouldn't wear a bra so that my sore nipples could air-dry and heal. As a result, I drenched T-shirt after T-shirt and always felt like I'd just come in from the rain. The light rubbing from the cotton shirts also irritated my nipples to no end. I tried nursing pads inside a stretchy sleep bra, but they pushed my nipples up or in—pure torture. I switched to wearing plastic shells over my nipples, tucked inside my bra, which worked for a while. Though I didn't have to deal with the irritation from my T-shirt, the shells quickly overflowed with milk.

All the while, I was trying to get my son to latch on. His gum grinding coupled with my nipple issues made feedings utterly agonizing. During this period, I made a brief visit to a friend's house to see her new baby, who'd been born soon after Aidan. I tried not to stare as her son sucked gently and efficiently in the football hold while she reclined on the couch, feet crossed on the coffee table.

"You're so lucky," I said.

The public health nurses who continued to visit me almost daily suggested that we rearrange my nursing station. We tried couch pillows, bed pillows, the Boppy nursing pillow—stuffed under my elbows and behind my back—and then no pillow at all. My feet went up on a chair, down on a stack of books, sideways on the couch. I was too hot, too lopsided, too tense. Nothing helped.

Weeks passed. Outside, temperatures reached the upper eighties. Inside, where I remained nursing—or trying to—around the clock, several of the windows of my apartment had been painted shut by an inept house painter. I felt like a potato baking in my living room. While some mothers wear makeup and brush their hair for their homecoming photos, I did neither for weeks. Instead, I readjusted the numerous plastic barrettes plastering back my hair. I never even thought to put in my contacts, and big, dark circles appeared beneath my eyes. I was a sweaty, dirty, exhausted, stressed-out mess—and Joanne, Fairbanks's only hands-on lactation consultant, got used to seeing me that way.

One day in late July, I left the front door unlocked and struggled to put on a clean, dry shirt while Aidan sat quietly in the bouncer seat.

Joanne arrived, and her calm voice eased my tension. "How's Aidan doing? How're you?"

She left her shoes at the door and joined Aidan and me in the living room. A woman my age, Joanne wore jeans and a collared shirt, her public health badge dangling from a shoelace around her neck. She crouched next to the bouncer. He'd started to whimper. "Hello, Mr. Aidan."

I took Aidan in my arms, and Joanne helped layer me with pillows. I then tried—and failed—to latch Aidan onto my breast. Defeat burrowed deep inside me. Aidan was trying, but he still hadn't caught on.

Joanne rubbed my shoulder, triggering my self-pity. The pain, the weariness, the frustration—it all welled up inside me, catching in my throat. I had tried for so long. Now I felt like a failure. Why couldn't I do this simple, age-old task? Why couldn't I feed my baby like millions of mothers before me? What was wrong with me?

As if reading my mind, Joanne said, "You're a great mother, Mary Jo. Most women would've given up by now. You're such a strong woman."

I looked at her, chewing the inside of my cheek to keep from sobbing.

She squeezed my shoulder again, as if to underscore her words. "You are."

A few tears escaped, and I wiped them away. Aidan had to learn this. He would. But that day seemed so far away.

All this time, however, Aidan was growing, and so was his tiny mouth. He got stronger. We made adjustments. He started to move his tongue more freely inside his mouth, and I even saw it touch his lower lip once or twice.

Finally, at about five weeks old, we got suction . . . clearly, definitively. I looked at Joanne kneeling on the floor next to me. "I think he's latched on," I said.

After that, sometimes it took Joanne and her expertise to get Aidan to latch on correctly. Other times, I could do it myself, but it usually took five or six tries. Sometimes, he didn't get the "fish lips" right and his bottom lip got stuck inside his mouth. Other times, his body angle hurt me. But we worked at it. We kept practicing. And Aidan started to gain weight, rapidly. So fast, in fact, that the nurses couldn't believe it: twelve ounces in one week, a whole pound the next.

By the time Aidan was six and a half weeks old, he was a different baby. He could nurse, no help required. My engorged breasts had deflated, and though I still tucked cabbage leaves in my bra and downed peppermint Altoids to slow my overabundant milk supply, I was much more confident about nursing and pain-free. Finally. I wept with relief.

"You worked so hard, Mary Jo," Joanne said at her last home visit. Aidan had just turned seven weeks. "He has a beautiful latch. Some mothers don't want to give up nursing after such a struggle." She raised her eyebrows.

"I'm shooting for a year," I said, cradling Aidan, his eyes closed, his hand resting on my breast. "Maybe longer."

Aidan is now almost nine months old, and we're still going strong. His tongue regularly stretches past his lips. And he loves nursing.

I used to think of breastfeeding as a battle between Aidan and me. But it wasn't. Aidan and I were always on the same side. And we still are.

Mary Jo Marcellus Wyse

Light of My Life

I'm in our tiny bathroom talking to myself in the mirror. *Can this be?* I ask.

Still rocking with the tide, I nod back at me. Though I've never given birth before, I'm starting to understand how this goes. It's like they all said: you just have to go with it.

I knew it would happen today. We'd even waited until this afternoon to do our artful pregnancy photos. One final hour of intimacy, the two of us for the last time like this. Laughing at the ridiculous sheet we picked to make it look discreet, when my ripe-fruit roundness was perfect as it was. Trying out stupid poses and making shadows on the wall with the bump. By the time we got bored, the twinges had already begun.

We took a final walk to the park behind our flat. The sea glistened in the distance, and the sunset-colored leaves shone in the autumn sun. Dogs ran, and the homeless man with his hundred black sacks caught my eye and smiled as I carried my shifting secret inside. We'd never see any of this with the same eyes again. Tomorrow, we'll be parents. I'll be a mother. I'm ready. Or at least I think I am.

It takes time to find the rhythm that holds me true during labor; keeping it is even trickier. I try to relax my mind, to unplug it from the planet, to trust this clever body instead. I can do it. I know I can do it.

Deep in the night, I create my space in the bedroom. The streetlights stream through the gap in the curtains over my bare body as I sway at the end of our iron bed. I keep the world out by closing my eyes. Images stream behind them—the sea blasting at rocks, castles, forests, long stone corridors, white sails. It could be curtains or it could be people in white robes flowing at either side of me.

It feels like my time could be near, but rather than letting it happen, I escape to the bathroom. The contrast of the overhead light and the gray tiles and grasping hold of the cold towel rail bring me out of myself to the decision that this hurts. It stings like salt water. The thinking and deciding make it hurt more.

The thoughts come thick and fast now, can't stop them. Can't stop myself from grabbing the clock to see how long this has been going on (twelve hours and counting), from wondering what Dom's doing (filling the birth pool with hot water from the kettle).

I stumble back to the dark bedroom, still niggling at myself. I just need another pillow, another sip of water, another remedy, another way to avoid this—the raging rapids of the life force. But as someone once said, this is not Disneyland. And the ride ain't gonna stop for me, no matter how hard I swim against it.

I think I'm getting it now.

I reach for a touchstone. I think about all the women birthing now, those who birthed before me. I think about letting birth work through me. I think about a cave and the sea whooshing through it . . . ah, okay, there it is . . . and I flow with that. And that's how it goes. The flowing, the feeling, the moments of calming insight mixed with cold moments of struggle, fight, and fear in the bathroom. Regardless, the night beats on, my body beats on, my baby beats on. And soon I will meet him.

The long night disappears somewhere. Morning is here, but the baby isn't.

"Okay, sweetie?" Dom asks me.

No, I'm not. I sob sorry salty tears. I'm beat and I don't want to be a birthing goddess. I want my mum. I phone the hospital and beg to please send the reinforcements. But the hospital isn't interested.

"It's not time, dear. Get in the pool. Get some sleep."

I slide into the steaming water for the first time— and mercy! I experience the most gratifying relief of my entire life. I'm held up, the liquid absorbs my tensions, soothing heat caresses my swollen body. I gratefully surrender to it and begin to cry—wail, really—letting go of myself. That's when it finally happens. I'd forgotten what they'd told me about the inland sea. The waters come rushing down and with them my baby's head, hot and sharp and ready to be born.

But I am not ready. I cling to one last shred, hold on by my fingernails. I tell myself I need to wait for the midwife.

It's an eternity before she arrives and says what I already know: it's time to push. Now. But even when I try, something holds me back. I may not be on the planet at that moment, but I clearly hear her say, "You've got ten minutes, and if he's not out, you're going in an ambulance."

I think not.

Me, the one I really am, steps up now. I become focused, bring my hands to prayer, squat down into the water like a pregnant Buddha, and appear to go inside myself completely. I am not aware of this; Dom will tell me afterward. In this moment, there is no me, no body, no pool. There is just everything—the whole, the one, the all. And light, exploding. Then, there is him—the sleek pup plunging into the water below me, shimmering to the surface into my arms, fleshy and luminous and real. And the world rushes back again, and I soar in behind it, incandescent with my joy.

Soon, it is quiet in the sunny bedroom, and I am smiling like a proud fool as my son latches on and feeds from my left breast. He is perfect and plump, downy and delicious. I hold him close to my heart. I am all heart. Gabriel, my light bringer, my miracle maker, is here.

Anna Packham

This story was first published in The Mother Magazine *(United Kingdom), July 2008.*

Power Eating

Being a first-time mom is hard enough, but when you have twins and they are born extremely prematurely, it takes the concept to a whole new level. Not only do you have to learn about motherhood, but you also have to survive a crash course in pediatric medicine.

I am a doctor, so the medical part actually seemed far less monumental than the mothering. I understood machines and medicines but had no idea how to hold a baby or change a diaper. I sincerely hoped that maternal instinct wasn't just some overused catch phrase, because I'd had no younger brothers or sisters to practice on growing up and I'd made it a rule never to baby-sit any child who still needed help with bodily functions. I was a complete novice.

But a couple of months into the twins' stay in the neonatal intensive care unit, after I'd muddled through many inelegant diaper changes and learned how to hold my babies despite the tubes and machines, I began to feel more comfortable with the motherhood part of the equation. So I announced to the medical team, "I want my boys to try a bottle."

They had been fed for weeks and weeks by a tube down the nose, receiving a special high-calorie formula. My body, too shocked and sick, had refused to cooperate in producing any milk. I was beginning to feel like I couldn't do anything right. I couldn't stay pregnant for nine months, I couldn't make milk, and I couldn't even change a diaper correctly. But I was convinced I would be able to do one thing successfully: feed them.

When I first brought up the idea of bottle-feeding my boys, I was told the feeding tubes are often needed for months, because babies born so prematurely typically lack the coordination and strength to both suck and swallow. The stress of being that sick so early in life seems to slow the progress even more, so many preemies go home with these feeding tubes. The answer was a gentle but firm, "Not yet."

I laughed. And it wasn't because I was delusional from lack of sleep, although that would have been a valid reason for such a seemingly out-of-place reaction. After all, my two boys had been born almost four months early, each weighing just over one and a half pounds. They'd spent weeks on machines to help them breathe, received medications so they could live, and one even had complicated heart surgery. Shock and stress were my constant companions—but not the reason for my chuckle.

I laughed because, while I was willing to admit that I knew very little about motherhood, I did know a thing or two about eating. My whole life has revolved around food and my pursuit of the next meal. No matter how I'm feeling, physically or emotionally, I can always eat; in fact, it usually seems like the best option in any given situation. I am not fickle; salty or sweet will do the trick. Recently, I heard about a chocolate bar that is mixed with bacon. I shook my head in awe of the wicked genius that dreamed up the brilliant combination, and then quickly wondered where I might get one for myself.

Unfortunately, this carnal desire has also contributed to my lifelong obsession with those thirty pounds that stand between me and a pair of size-ten jeans, now gathering dust in the bottom drawer. I feel as if I have been on one continuous (and unsuccessful) diet or the other since the age of seventeen. Despite knowing the calorie count, fat content, and fiber grams for practically every food in existence, I am doomed to fail because I am already dreaming of lunch during breakfast and of dinner during lunch.

Some may blame their weight on a slow metabolism, but not me. I embrace the horror; I just love to eat.

As a doctor I theorize that there is some evolutionary advantage to this wanton ability, a genetic vestige from the days when we hunted saber-toothed tigers and mastodon, and that it is not a sign of gluttony. Sure, fast-food restaurants and grocery stores are mere minutes away and my fridge is well-stocked, but theoretically, famine could happen, and if it does, I am prepared. My husband shares this ability, so I surmised that my boys would be doubly blessed. It just did not seem possible to me that any child of ours would have any difficulty whatsoever taking to food.

The medical team humored my long-winded anthropological theories, but I knew they secretly thought I had lost it. I pestered incessantly, and they gave in a week before they normally allow a baby to try a bottle. Even my husband, who had been gung ho about bottle-feeding the boys at first, was getting tired of hearing me explain my complicated treatise on eating and genetics.

Deep down, I desperately wanted something, just one thing, to be less complicated, because so far, everything else had been such a fight. Given my feelings about food, it just seemed like an obvious place for success. And for the first time, I actually heard my mother's intuition kick in, screaming, "Give them the damn bottle!"

I understood the hesitation of the medical team. A premature baby suffers through so many hardships, and as a parent, you suffer right along with them. For every two steps forward, there is almost always one or more steps backward. It is hard to keep piling on the disappointment. So my insistence that they try a bottle earlier than planned probably seemed like the perfect setup. But the mother in me had been unleashed, and I realized that I actually knew my boys—and they were ready.

After much pleading and cajoling, we had the go-ahead. My heart was beating like a drum. Oliver was first, and I held my breath when, for an instant, it seemed as if he weren't quite sure what to do. But when the first drop of formula finally hit his tongue, a look I know so well—what we call "chocolate euphoria"—came over his face. "What were you waiting for?" he seemed to implore with his tiny features, and then promptly downed the bottle. His brother, Victor, as predicted, did exactly the same thing. Within three days, the feeding tubes were gone. The reaction from the staff was stunned disbelief, but I had known all along that my boys would outperform in this area. Mothers know these things.

Fast-forward five years. Oliver races into the kitchen, screaming, "Yummy, chicken!" when he hears me take the roast out of the oven. After eating both drumsticks, he promptly voices his displeasure that chickens don't have three legs. Victor prefers bacon and a nice fresh roll slathered with butter—and, really, who doesn't? Now when I reach for that last slice of pizza, it is like diving into a mosh pit of hands.

How ironic that the food demon with whom I had been locked in an epic love-hate battle for more than half of my life opened my eyes and proved to be the first of many amazing successes. I now view those size-ten jeans in an entirely different light. I used to wistfully take them out every once in a while, but as I've watched my sons grow and thrive, I have stopped opening the drawer. Being thin is one thing, but my family and I are built to survive, and those are the best genes of all.

Jennifer Gunter

Equal to the Task

"What's wrong? Why isn't she crying?" A swarm of doctors and nurses were in the delivery room, but no one would tell me anything. As soon as Emily had been delivered just moments before, they'd whisked her to the corner of the room. I lifted my head trying to see what was happening, holding on to a shred of hope—although I hadn't heard her cry, I thought I'd seen her move. She wouldn't move if she were dead, would she?

A nurse mumbled something about a respiratory therapist. In my postdelivery haze, I couldn't connect those words with any kind of meaning. The nurse walked over to me carrying a wrapped bundle. I was terrified she was going to place a dead baby in my arms. She laid the bundle on my belly and then took the oxygen mask from my face and put it on the baby. My heart raced and my hands shook as I struggled to sit up to get a closer look. She was beautiful. Her soft downy skin smelled like heaven, from where she had recently come.

"Is she okay?" I asked.

The nurse refused to look me in the eye and wouldn't give me a straight answer.

I held my baby for only a couple minutes before they took her away to prepare her for transport to a larger hospital. Emily was in severe respiratory distress, and the small hospital where I'd just given birth didn't have a newborn intensive care unit. The life-flight team came in and talked to me about what was happening and brought in Emily so I could tell her goodbye. She was all prepared to travel in an incubator, with an intravenous port in her head and an oxygen tube in her nose, so I couldn't hold her.

The paramedic looked at my husband, James, and said, "You can either ride with us or follow us, so you'll have a car."

James looked at me with a question in his eyes. Instantly, I knew he was torn, feeling like he should stay and take care of me but desperately wanting to go with the baby.

With tears in my eyes, I said. "Go. I don't want her to be alone."

He squeezed my hand and asked, "Are you sure?"

"She needs someone with her who loves her," I said, and looked down, unable to look him in the face any longer. I wanted to be the one going with her.

My husband left, and I was alone to face the most solitary night of my life. All around me, I heard the sounds of babies and pictured other mothers cuddling, nursing, and bonding with their babies. My empty arms ached. I had delivered Emily at almost midnight, so I should have been tired, but I couldn't sleep. I couldn't stop thinking about my sweet baby and how she needed me and how I couldn't be there for her. I still wasn't sure if she would even be okay. For all I knew, the last time I would see her alive was when I had reached in the transport incubator and held her tiny hand.

At dawn, the morning light shone through my window, but it brought no light into my heart. I had never felt so isolated. It was as though the world was going on around me and I could only watch. The nursing staff had not even come in to check on me very often. Later, when I was discharged, I realized that a sign indicating that I wouldn't be taking a baby home with me had been posted outside my door. Apparently, this unhappy circumstance made people feel like I needed to be left alone, but I would have loved to have had some company.

Finally, the hospital grief counselor came in to see me. I talked about my despair, which was unlike anything I'd ever felt before. Helpless, anxious, and trapped didn't even begin to describe my feelings. Physically, I felt terrible, but it was nothing compared to my anguish over not being with my baby and not even knowing how she was doing.

When the counselor asked me if there was anything he could do to help, I broke down. I told him that I was desperate to find out the condition of my baby and that I'd been calling my husband's phone throughout the night, but he wasn't answering. He agreed to call a counselor at the other hospital and try to track down my husband.

A short while later, the phone by my bedside rang. I struggled to turn over and reach it. "Hello?"

"Hi. How are you?" James asked.

Hot tears came to my eyes at the sound of his familiar voice. "Where have you been? I've been calling all morning," I said in an exasperated tone of voice.

"I've been with Emily. They had to put her on a ventilator, because she couldn't breathe on her own, even with the oxygen."

"Is she going to be okay?"

"Yes, I think she will. She's stable now," he said, sighing as if he were extremely tired.

"Please come get me." I started sobbing, no longer able to hold back the tears.

"You can't leave yet, can you?" he asked.

"I have to. I'm going crazy here. Emily needs me, and I can't bear to be away from her any longer."

The nurse on duty strongly recommended that I stay in the hospital at least one more night, but I couldn't do it. I had to be with my baby. Nine hours after giving birth, I checked myself out of the hospital and made the twenty-minute drive to the other hospital with my husband.

As I rode the elevator up to the fourth floor, my heart thudded with anticipation. I couldn't wait to see Emily. I couldn't bring a picture of her to my mind, but I could still remember her scent. It would be forever imprinted on my memory.

After walking through both sets of double doors into the NICU, I washed up, scrubbing my hands and arms. Then I approached her tiny bed. She was in an open Isolette so the medical staff could keep a close watch on her. It was hard to see her precious face because of all the tubing and wires. The ventilator tube stuck out of her mouth and made her little chest constantly flutter. It was difficult for me to watch.

My arms ached to hold her, but her condition was too unstable. Even the slightest touch was too stimulating. I spent the entire day by her bedside, unable to take my eyes off her. In my current frame of mind, I couldn't even worry about my five other children at home. Fortunately, family was taking care of them so that I could focus all my energy on Emily.

When nighttime came, I didn't want to leave her. The thought of my child, especially one so helpless and tiny, being alone in the hospital about killed me.

I didn't get much sleep that night. Every two hours, I had to get up and use a breast pump to help my milk come in, because Emily couldn't breastfeed. I thought of her the entire night, hoping and praying she was okay.

By six o'clock, I was up and ready to leave, even though visiting hours didn't start until eight. I couldn't wait to get to the hospital.

When I arrived, the nurse was just getting ready to feed Emily and asked me if I would like to do it. The "feeding" consisted of slowly depressing a syringe filled with a special formula into a tube that went into her nose and down to her stomach. I was ecstatic to finally be able to do something for my baby. One of the major things bothering me was that I hadn't been able to do anything for her. Now, I could at least feed my baby.

After Emily had been on the ventilator for a little more than seventy-two hours, the respiratory therapist checked her and said she could be taken off. She was moved to a "head box," basically a clear plastic box placed over her head that oxygen was pumped into. I was hoping that, without the ventilator, they would let me hold her, but it still wasn't time.

A few days later, Emily was taken out of the head box and put on a regular oxygen tube. As soon as the nurse finished inserting the tube into Emily's nose, she turned to me and asked, "Would you like to hold her?"

I didn't think I had heard her correctly. The day had finally come. Ever since they had taken her out of my arms the night she was born, I had dreamed about this moment. With tears shining in my eyes, I said, "I would love to."

I was nervous. Even though I had five other children, I had never held a baby so small and fragile. The nurse swaddled Emily tightly in a blanket and handed her to me. I was sitting in the rocking chair where I had held my silent vigil by her bedside the last several days. I kissed her on the cheek. Her skin was velvety soft and smelled so new and clean. It was a reverent moment I will never forget, as I realized that I had been entrusted this special spirit to raise and care for. I hoped I was equal to the task. I held

Emily for a long time, until my husband got impatient and wanted a turn. I was afraid to let her go and didn't want the moment to end.

During the week, I got to participate in most of Emily's daily care and experienced other important firsts: changed her diaper and clothing for the first time, bathed her for the first time, and nursed her for the first time.

Throughout Emily's three-week hospital stay, we were very aware that she was being watched over by her Father in Heaven. When the time came to take her home, the doctor came by on her daily rounds. She said that something just didn't feel right and decided to keep Emily another day. At that point, Emily had been off oxygen for a couple of days. Before a newborn with RDS could be discharged, the hospital requires that the baby pass a car seat test. The test involves measuring the infant's oxygen levels while the baby sits in a car seat for thirty minutes. Emily did not pass the test; her oxygen kept dropping too low.

The doctor decided to put her back on oxygen, explaining that we had taken too many steps at once and it had set Emily's progress back some. After she'd been taken off oxygen two days earlier, we had started increasing her feedings quite rapidly because she was doing so well with breastfeeding. Until then, most of her nutrition had come from the feeding tube in her nose. It turned out that, when she started breastfeeding in earnest, she spent so much energy eating that she wasn't able to keep up her oxygen level.

Emily came home a few days later with a heart monitor, a respiratory monitor, and still on oxygen. She ended up needing the oxygen for four months, so it was a blessing that the doctor was inspired not to send her home without it.

Since then, we have helped Emily through other firsts: her first smile, first tooth, first step, and first word. She is turning five this year and will be going to kindergarten, and I'm afraid that her first day of school will be tear-filled for me. She is the light of my life and I'm so blessed to have her in it. Of course, many more firsts are ahead. And I pray every day that I will continue to be equal to the task.

Kimberly Thompson

The Big Blowout

"Houston," I said from the back seat, "we have a problem."

I was in my parents' beautiful Cadillac, and we had just pulled up in front of their new house in a very nice subdivision for retirees. Their home was almost finished being built, and we were coming out to take a look at the progress.

My dad turned off the engine and opened his door, while my mother turned around in the passenger seat to see what I was talking about. "What's the matter, dear?" she asked.

I leaned over to my two-year-old son and almost threw up as the murky odor filled the air. "Mom," I said, holding my breath, "why don't you go on in? I'll change him, and we'll meet you inside in a minute."

She gladly agreed and exited the stench-filled car. I casually picked up the diaper bag and then glanced over at my pride and joy. My son looked at me sweetly and smiled, seeming particularly pleased with his special work.

No biggie, I thought. *I'll just lay him on the back seat and change him quickly.*

It was late January, so I had several layers of clothing to deal with. I took off his Stride Rite sneakers and tossed them on the floor. I unbuckled his seatbelt, helped him out of his jacket and laid it down on the seat. Then I laid him on top of his jacket and unbuttoned his corduroy pants.

As I pulled off his pants, a trail of dark filth traveled down his legs onto the jacket, the clean diaper that I was planning to change him into, the ivory leather of the back seat of my parents' car, my hands, my pants, and everything else in sight. My boy had had a major blowout! The poop was running out both sides of the diaper. I couldn't believe it. The amount of poop was astonishing. I'm not kidding. Poop was literally everywhere!

I frantically grabbed for the diaper bag, spilling the contents all over the back floorboard. I was one of those moms who was always prepared for the worst. I usually brought just about everything in the nursery with me wherever I went . . . except for this day, of course. I searched through the contents on the floor, looking for a clean diaper, some wipes, and some hand sanitizer.

Everything I touched seemed to be covered in poop. It's like the stuff was appearing out of thin air and multiplying on contact. It was horrifying. How could so much poop come out of one tiny human being? It just wasn't natural.

I continued searching through the myriad of baby products until I finally found the travel-size diaper wipes—only to flip it open and find it empty. Yikes! I kicked through everything else on the floor with the toe of my boot, searching for another clean diaper to use as a wipe. There wasn't one. How could this be?

Unfortunately, as I got more and more agitated, so did my son. It was freezing out there in the car, and now he was crying. Completely overwhelmed, I couldn't help myself and started crying too. Then my son upped the ante and started screaming. I felt so helpless. He wouldn't hold still, so he was smearing more poop on more things every time he moved.

I opened the door to the car, and frigid air rushed in as I yelled out for my parents. "I need some help!"

They were at the back of the house, so they couldn't hear me. I was frustrated, anxious, cold, and let's face it, downright stinky. I tried again.

"Mom! Dad! Help me!"

Thankfully, my mother heard me this time and came flying around the side of the house like a super hero. I'm surprised her cape didn't get caught in the tree as she came whooshing to my rescue. She came right in and took over for me. It was nothing short of amazing.

She opened the trunk of her car, grabbed two towels, a plastic bag, and a container of anti-bacterial wipes. This lady was prepared! She pulled me out of the back seat, thrusting several wipes along with a box of tissues into my hands. "Go on," she urged me. "Get yourself cleaned up, and I'll take care of him."

I tried to get the poop off of me but succeeded only in spreading it around even more. I felt pure panic, like I was under attack, like I was the star of a Stephen King movie. My preference would be a Lifetime movie with a happy ending. My fantasy world was quickly being crushed by the real world.

At last, I finally got my hands clean, but my shirt and pants were a total disaster.

I watched in wonder as my mother scooped up my son and took him around to the front of the car. (Mind you, she was able to do this without getting any poop on herself.) She stood my son up in the front seat, stripped him of his soiled clothes, cleaned him up, and wrapped him first in one of my Dad's old

T-shirts and then in a blanket, both clean, of course. She sat him down, gave him a baby book to look at, closed the passenger door, and then came around to the terrible mess in the back seat.

In a matter of minutes, she had everything sparkling clean. Well, everything but me, that is. My shirt and pants were still covered in poop, and there were no extra clothes for me to change into.

"Not to worry, dear," Mom said calmly. "We'll just head back home and get you all cleaned up too."

She went inside to tell Dad that we needed to go home. He took one look at me and burst out laughing. I guess I was quite a sight. My makeup was running down my face, my hair was a disheveled mess, and my clothes were covered in filth. I didn't smell too rosy, either.

As Dad reached up and wiped a smudge off my left cheek with his hankie, he said simply, "Welcome to motherhood."

Susan Lynn Perry

Cordless

"Mom, how will Gabey get out of your belly?" asks Micayla, my four-year-old, as we fight traffic on a snowy December afternoon.

My face cringes. "Well, uh, um . . ." I always strive to be truthful with my daughter, but I'm not sure her young mind is ready for the details of childbirth. I fiddle with the radio, trying to look busy, until I can come up with an answer. "Gabe will keep growing in my tummy until he's big enough to come out and . . . uh . . . then, uh . . ."

"Do they cut your belly open and take him out?" Micayla asks, her voice filled with a somewhat disturbing excitement about this possibility.

Apparently, my womb is not the most baby-friendly environment, so the likelihood of my needing a cesarean section is low. When I was pregnant with Micayla, I was on bed rest for the last three months to make sure she didn't come too soon. Now, at seven months' gestation with Gabe, the warning signs of preterm labor are becoming apparent. I have trouble keeping my kids in, not getting them out. But how do I describe the alternate exit strategy to a preschooler?

"Uh, yeah. That's one way babies come out of their mommies' tummies." Color begins returning to my face.

"So how do they close up your belly?"

Agh! I'm not off the hook. But, before I can answer, the voice in the backseat pipes up again.

"Do they close it up with duct tape?"

Okay, I know two wrongs don't make a right, but I'm desperate to end this conversation before I have to explain the birds and the bees to a preschooler. I nod my head.

"So they cut you open, pull Gabey out, put tape across your belly, and that's how you have a baby?" Her enthusiasm rivals that of being at Chuck E. Cheese, her favorite pizza joint.

I could go for broke and tell my third lie, but my conscience begins kicking in, inadvertently drawing me further into this conversation. "First they have to cut the cord."

"Whaaaaat?" she shrieks, almost causing me to hit another car. "They aren't going to cut my baby brother's cord! I'm going to say, 'No, you may not hurt my brother. You can't cut his cord.'" Her words are so forceful that I don't even need to look to know her finger is wagging all over the place.

A giggle threatens to escape my mouth. It is too comical to realize that my daughter—typically a mama's girl to the bone—is perfectly fine with me being sliced open and crudely duct-taped back together yet is overly concerned about her unborn brother.

"But, Micayla, they have to cut the cord," I explain. "That's part of how babies are born."

"No! I won't let them."

"But it won't even hurt him," I plead.

"Yes, it will!"

If you've ever engaged in a battle with a four-year-old, especially my four-year-old, you know it's a hopeless cause. I'm tempted to pull out the "I'm the mom and I said so" card and tell her not to worry about it, but her tiny reflection in the rearview mirror reveals her despondency.

I draw in a long breath and let it out slowly. "Sunshine, the cord isn't really part of Gabe. It's just something that goes from my belly to his to give him food. They'll cut it far away from him where he won't even feel it."

"I don't want them cutting it." The edge to her voice is strong and full of conviction.

"They cut yours, and you're okay."

For a moment, there is silence in the back seat. "But . . ."

"Besides, if they don't cut the cord, Gabe will always have to be really close to me. How could we drive anywhere, since the cord wouldn't reach all the way to his car seat?"

A slight glimmer of understanding appears in her eyes.

"Just think about what life would be like if they hadn't cut your cord. You wouldn't be able to watch your video downstairs every morning while I take a shower."

I've hit a nerve. A nearly unintelligible "not watch Barney?" ekes out after a gasp. She ponders my statement a minute and then turns it on me. "Yeah, well, you would get to go to school with me every day, so we could always be together. And you could sleep in my bed every single night."

"And you'd have to go to work with me. And help with all the cleaning. And go running with me. And . . ."

"Okay, okay. They can cut the cord," she says as giggles fill the car.

My son—who, with his sister's permission, has a belly button and not a permanent umbilical cord— is now a busy one-year-old. Micayla remains as concerned about his welfare today as she was while he was in utero. She "reads" books to him every day before naptime, despite the fact that her reading vocabulary consists of only a handful of words. When Gabe falls, Micayla rushes to his side and comforts him. She shares her sacred "peely" cheese (string cheese) and lets him play with her toys. She even wants to marry Gabe, knowing she should only marry someone if she loves him and Gabe is the only boy she loves.

What is more, Micayla's enhanced level of empathy has permeated into other relationships. She gets upset when she sees her cousins fighting, and she prays every night for anyone she knows who is sick.

Sometimes I wonder what might have happened had I put an immediate end to our talk on that cold winter afternoon. Would Micayla still have loved Gabe the way she does, or would my desire to avoid the uncomfortable have made her feel that she was wrong for wanting to protect and care for her brother? Would my words have caused her to be callous and distant from her sibling even before he was even born? I'm glad I made the choice I did, for, although a cord was cut, an even stronger bond was formed.

Stacy Voss

Learning to Breathe

My water broke September 11, 2001, as I kept watch over the Golden Gate Bridge out my bedroom window, willing it not to fall next.

Amniotic fluid started leaking down my legs, and a clock started ticking with loud clanks—not my biological clock but a medical protocol clock that measured the risk of infection from the moment my water broke. Adrenaline in my system kept me from going into full labor. I didn't feel safe; I couldn't give birth. My planned gentle water birth in a freestanding birth center changed to induced labor hooked up to needles and tubes in the backup hospital. After many false starts and delays, my daughter was born at 9:23 A.M. on September 13, 2001.

All was not well, however. New little swimmer that she was, Sarah confused the mediums of water and air and took her first breath while still inside of me. She was in distress at birth, fluid filling places where only air should be. The midwives put her—an ashen gray—on my chest; the nurse held a tiny oxygen mask to her mouth. Sarah was full-term, ten pounds, and a solid weight on my body. I remember thinking that she didn't feel real, more like a cherub carved of slick, cool marble. My husband cut the cord, and then they took her from me, down the hall, into the infant ICU, where she, like me years before as a preemie baby and like me in the delivery room, was hooked up to wires, tubes, cords, and invaded by needles.

Sarah looked like an image from a science fiction movie. Tubes connected to needles stuck into her nearly transparent skin. Wires taped to a small silver heart on her chest led to a beeping and clicking machine. Her head and upper body shone with slick sweat under an oxygen tent. In the middle of all this technology, my newborn daughter tried to do something that comes so naturally to me that I'm not even aware I'm doing it. She struggled to breathe—too quickly, too shallowly, too unevenly.

Standing over her, I felt I had to make a connection. I needed to feel her. I reached out my hand and gently touched her leg. She jerked away at my touch. She didn't have enough force of air to make a real sound, but there was no doubt she was crying. Her face, red and tight, turned side to side as she tossed her head. Her hands made tight fists as she attempted to fight off invisible attackers. Her body, heavy with fat and muscle, shivered.

I stroked her legs gingerly, softly, and her thrashing slowed. She stopped attempting to cry. But I will never forget that she thought the human touch, her mother's touch, would bring pain. I will never forget that she was alone under that oxygen tent, without comfort. I will never forget the silence of her cry. And I will never forget the weight on my lungs, my heart, and my soul as I stood over the new daughter I could not hold. As she and I struggled to breathe together in air newly rarified by her presence, I began to have faith in the continual breathing in and breathing out. In. Out. In. Out. Breathing together was enough.

Five days later, they released her from the infant intensive care, and she came home with us, healthy, happy, and new. But the fiery crashes, the dual collapses of water and buildings, that labor, those five days, would not leave me alone. They haunted my new-mother joy with fear-tinged razors. I wasn't sure how to be a mother in a world that seemed too tainted for my daughter's beauty. The untimely collapse of the World Trade Center towers and the early rupture of my membranes became inextricably intertwined in my imagination, and I couldn't think of one without the other. Yet, I couldn't fully remember either.

Maybe that is how memory works, picking up the

pieces around a trauma or a tragedy, because coming at it in a full frontal attack makes the scattered shards skitter away. I attempt to piece the slivers together, but like a broken mirror, they reflect back a changed image. I don't recognize what I see in the mirror. *Is this how it happened?* I think. *Is this really how it happened?*

Today, my daughter is six years old, and as I think back to that first year of motherhood, the Twin Towers loom less ominously. I reclaim the beautiful pieces— the ones that might not be as drama-filled or newsworthy: Waking next to my sleeping infant. Rocking her as she nursed. Her soft hand on my cheek. I leave the pieces that highlight the national trauma to the side now, and I know that my new-mother fear was just as much an illusion as the image in the broken mirror. Ultimately, my reality is what I make, I choose where to glue a broken piece, how to shape the repairs, how to make sense of the elements that memory offers me.

The Golden Gate Bridge did not fall, though it seemed like it would. My daughter is growing up to be a healthy, strong girl, though at the beginning I wasn't so sure. And I have grown into a confident mother and citizen who moves us smoothly through this chaotic and beautiful world, even though that seemed unlikely that first year. Surprisingly, learning to simply breathe in and out was, indeed, enough.

Amy Hudock

Nesting

From the minute I knew I was pregnant, I wanted my mom. She'd always been my closest friend and my best advisor on girl stuff. Oh yeah, we had our battles in my teen years—all part of the necessary breaking away. Yet, now that I was in my midtwenties, I felt like a scared little kid who needed Mommy.

My widowed mother had an overwhelming job as a business executive at a Seattle hotel. That placed her nearly 600 miles from the small Montana town that my husband and I called home. I knew it would be a challenge for her to break free long enough to provide the comforting reassurance I needed. But I hoped that she could be with us for the baby's birth.

Though John and I were excited by the tiny miracle I carried inside, we knew almost nothing about children. We'd planned to remain childless because we felt inept around kids. However, our relationship had become stale and empty without a family to nurture. So John quit his stressful job and found work in a Montana hamlet—an ideal place to raise a family. I chose to quit working so I could dedicate myself to motherhood—a job that seemed far more challenging than anything I'd ever done.

Needing all the support Mom could give, I called her as soon as possible.

"Mom, I'm pregnant!" I announced anxiously. "The baby's due October eighth. Help!"

"Honey, I'm so excited for you!" Mom replied. "But I can't be there on your due date. I'm in charge of a celebrity party that week. I'm so sorry."

My heart sank. Being pregnant was scary for both me and John. We'd just begun to make friends in our new hometown, and having no family or close friends around us, we felt alone. Who'd advise us on all the practical details of pregnancy, childbirth, and baby care? In my mind, no book, no class, and no stranger could give better advice than my mother.

"Tell you what," Mom continued, sensing my desperation, "as soon as my big event is over, I'll be there for yours. How's that? The baby will be late, anyway; you'll see. Nine days past due is typical for a firstborn. I can be there by then. Besides, that's six months away; I don't have to wait that long to come visit you. What if your sister and I drive over next month? I could take off a couple days in May."

"Okay, Mom," I said glumly.

My spirits lifted when Mom and Bette arrived five weeks later, bringing a little dresser loaded with baby clothes, blankets, and supplies. They'd collected nearly everything we needed for our new baby. Plus, Mom and Bette gave me lectures on taking my vitamins, eating right, and getting enough exercise. They spent hours telling us stories about pregnancy and babies. We took long walks, laughed, and commiserated for a couple days. Then they were gone. John and I were alone again.

John worked nights and slept until early afternoon. His schedule only added to my loneliness. We attended as many baby classes as we could, including training in natural birth techniques, breastfeeding, and basic infant care. Yet, we still felt inadequate.

As my October due date drew near, John's mother came to be with us. It was sweet of her to come, but Mom Bradford seemed to think of childbirth as a barely tolerable event. She felt awkward speaking about it, which left me feeling more anxious than ever. My heart ached to see my own spunky, "can-do" mother, who had endless stories about the joys and challenges of bringing children into the world. My due date came and went, with no hint of baby's arrival. Mom Bradford had obligations at home, so she left. We were on our own again.

Then the phone rang. My mother was able to break free from work a few days early. She would have flown into nearby Butte, Montana, but she couldn't bear to leave her old collie in a kennel. She asked if she could bring him along. Lance had developed a limp, and she wanted to monitor his condition. This was typical of Mom. By her rulebook, you never abandoned your loved ones, especially when they were in trouble.

The next day, Mom hit the road with eleven-year-old Lance and a lot of determination. Twelve hours later, she stumbled into my house exhausted, turned her collie loose in the backyard, and crashed into bed. But the very next morning, she was up and ready to go. After all, we had a baby on the way. We had things to do. We had to stay in shape. For the next few days, we walked and talked and buzzed around the house getting everything ready. With Mom there, a comforting security settled over our home.

Early one morning, while John and I were attempting to sleep, I heard clattering noises coming from the kitchen. Mom was up to something—but what?

Not able to face her level of energy just yet, I slipped stealthily out of bed and headed into the bathroom for a long soak in a hot tub. My back was a bit sore. As I eased into the soothing water, I felt a slight tension in my abdomen. After a few seconds, it relaxed. I smiled to myself. Was this the day? It happened again . . . and again before I finished my comforting soak. I was in labor!

I emerged from the bathroom all aglow, ready to tell Mom what was happening, but I wasn't ready for the chaos in my kitchen. It looked like a tornado had hit! The tornado was Mom.

She jumped up from scrubbing the floor and hugged me as I entered the room. A smell of disinfectant permeated the air. Cabinets were open to dry, with their contents scattered everywhere. The stove and refrigerator were open, their freshly washed parts carefully set out to dry.

"What are you doing?" I asked.

"Nesting," Mom answered excitedly as she gazed with pride at her work. "I've disinfected the entire nursery. Now I'm working on the kitchen. When John awakens, I'll vacuum the carpets and . . ."

"Mom, with all the racket you're making, it'll be a wonder if he isn't awake already. What is all this? What is 'nesting'?" I asked.

"It's something a woman does before her baby is born. You're going to have the baby today!" she announced in a perky voice. "I just know it, so I'm nesting."

"What? How do you know that? And shouldn't I be the one doing this nesting thing? After all, I'm the one having the baby."

"My goodness, you're in labor, aren't you?" Mom urged. "Aren't you?" Seeing a grin spread across my face, she shrieked, "I knew it! You are! Woo hoo!" as she did a little dance.

"Shush!" I scolded, laughing at Mom's antics. "Let John sleep. The labor isn't hard yet, only a gentle, rhythmic tension now and then. It could be false labor, you know."

In order to muffle her enthusiastic shouts, Mom slapped one hand over her mouth, though a few squeals still escaped.

"You're impossible," I said as I rolled my eyes.

"Nine days overdue, just as I thought," Mom teased. "It's the classic number of days for a first child, you know."

"Yes, Mom," I moaned. "You're hopeless. But we have to be quiet. John needs to sleep. Besides, I'm hungry. Where's all our food?"

Mom quickly cobbled together a nourishing meal for me. Thanking her, I settled down to eat, while she continued her flurry of "nesting" activities around me, refusing to quit until everything was tidy. She jabbered excitedly as she worked.

"I figured out what's wrong with Lance," she said. "His paw is swollen this morning. It's infected."

Seeing an opportunity to keep the house quiet for John, I suggested, "After I have breakfast, let's take Lance to the vet."

"What? We should be tending to you, not the dog," Mom insisted.

"No, Mom. I'm fine. It's too soon to go to the hospital. I'm not in any discomfort. Let's get old Lance's problem under control first." I couldn't believe my level of calm. I'd been so nervous about childbirth. Suddenly I was acting like a pro. All it took was Mom by my side. How I thanked God for her presence.

After everything was in order and sterilized, we took Lance to the veterinarian's office. Mom couldn't help announcing that I was in labor. I blushed repeatedly as the vet teased me about being at the wrong doctor's office.

"You know, we only deliver puppies, calves, and colts here. If you're carrying one of those, feel free to stay."

We ran a few errands on the way home. Each place we stopped Mom announced, "We're having a baby today!" as she pointed to my bulging abdomen. Everyone asked why I wasn't at the hospital, but I assured them I'd be okay. After all, I'd brought my security blanket . . . Mom was with me.

By the time we got home, John was up. He was elated to hear the news. Immediately, he notified his employer that he wouldn't be in for work that night.

It was evening before the labor intensified to the point I felt I should go to the hospital. Once we were settled in a labor room, John surprised himself by doing a wonderful job as a birthing coach. He kept me focused and calm through the difficult part of labor.

After a few hours of work, our tiny miracle was born. Daniel arrived exactly nine days late, just as Mom predicted. She glowed as she declared, "Ten little fingers and ten little toes. Just right!" We all rejoiced over our perfect little boy.

Only two short days later, Mom's vacation was over. She'd had only a brief time to give me on-the-job training in bathing, breastfeeding, and clothing Daniel. Now it was time for her to go.

Afraid to say goodbye, I stood trembling on the sidewalk while Mom loaded old Lance and her baggage into the car. Then she turned to me as I cradled Daniel in my arms. Scooping up his tiny wriggling body, she held him close, nuzzled him nose to nose, and whispered a sweet goodbye. Dark glasses hid her tears as she slipped Daniel back into my arms, kissed me on the cheek, and settled into her driver's seat. She choked out a last farewell and started the car.

One arm waved wildly from the driver's window as Mom pulled away from the curb. Lance eagerly poked his long snout out the opened passenger window. And they were gone.

I considered how brave she was—driving hundreds of miles all alone to support me at this critical time. Yet, my admiration for her went far beyond that. When Mom was my age, she'd followed my dad from the East Coast to settle in Seattle. When we three children were born, Mom was thousands of miles from her own mother—a nurse. But she toughed it out . . . alone. Dad died when we were all very young, and Mom was left to raise us . . . alone. Yet, she came through it all like a champion. She told me that she was never truly alone. God helped her every step of the way.

As I gazed down the road, hugging Daniel close to me, I still felt overwhelmed, but I knew he and I would be fine. After all, God had given me everything I needed—an intuitive "nester" in my living example of a good mom.

Laura L. Bradford

Double Trouble

I n the middle of the night, I startled awake to find myself in the living room, sitting upright on the couch. Blinking, I looked down in the dim light to find a baby in the crook of each arm. I didn't remember getting up, scooping up the twins, or nursing them. However, there they lay, one on each side, slipping off into the drunken slumber of a warm, dry, and well-fed infant. I remembered my husband's response earlier that day when someone asked him how it was to have twins. "It's so fun!"

Huh? This is fun? I thought. *Maybe for him. He's sound asleep right now, and he'll be off to work in the morning. Sure, he helps bathe and dress them, but he doesn't spend eight hours every day and through the night just feeding them.*

I burped the babies and put them back into their crib. As I crawled back into my own bed, I hoped that autopilot was a safe way to handle newborns.

The morning brought the usual hullabaloo associated with getting my husband off to work and our three oldest children off to school. By the time the bus came, the twins and our three-year-old, Matthew, were up and needing attention. The morning melted away all too quickly in the heat of doing chores and caring for three small children. All too soon, it was time to bundle up the babies and take Matt to preschool. At least it wasn't my day to be a parent helper. Today, I could drop him off and bring the twins home for their nap.

It seemed like a rare treat. Matt's preschool time was also my only chance to run errands and do the shopping with only the two small babies in tow. Going to the store had become an even more time-intensive task than usual since the twins had been born. Every new mother knows that perfect strangers feel welcome to talk to you and admire the baby. Taking twins to a public place compounds the phenomenon. Every third person stops and wants to talk. There is no such thing as a quick trip to the store with such a conversation starter in your cart!

On this day, during the two hours after dropping off Matt, I had nursed the twins and put them down for a nap, done the dishes, and swept the floor. With no energy left to tidy up, I flopped back on that same couch and looked down at my little ones sleeping on a blanket laid out on the floor. How I yearned to curl up and doze off myself, but soon I would have to bundle them into their car seats to go pick up their brother. Their peaceful faces seemed to mock my weariness as I watched them slumber.

The realization of the sacrifices of motherhood invaded my mind. Someone had given me a spoon rest as a wedding gift that sported the sentiment, "For this I spent four years in college?" I looked around at the clutter left by my kids as they'd prepared for school that morning, the pile of cloth diapers on the other end of the couch waiting to be folded, and the toys scattered around the room. It seemed that I spent all of my waking hours nursing and caring for children. After last night, I had to admit that I spent part of my sleeping hours caring for them, too. Someone always needed something from me. Feeding, clothing, and nurturing six children seemed a demanding and thankless job at that moment.

Shopping, cooking, and doing dishes for two adults and four children is daunting enough without adding nursing two babies, sometimes both together, sometimes one at a time. If I switched to bottles, my husband would willingly help feed the girls in the evenings. However, I couldn't ask him to get up with them at 3:00 A.M., because he couldn't do his job safely without a good night's sleep. Besides, I was determined to give the twins the same benefits I felt my other babies had gained from being suckled. Sometimes, though, I wondered if the closeness or even the nutrition was worth the time and energy drain it took with two.

Then I realized that if feeding everyone were my only concern, I could handle it better, but they all needed to be clothed, too. I had always said that a new baby doubles a family's laundry. Somehow, that was true even of my third and fourth babies. With six of us, there had been a mountain of laundry. Now, with double the diapers, outfits, and blankets to wash, the laundry had become Mount Everest. It was never all clean, folded, and put away.

Those few minutes on the couch would be the only rest I got all day. Not long after I picked Matt up from preschool, the older kids would clamber off the bus and into the house. School papers and stories would fill the time until their dad came home and shared the events of his day. With his help, dinner, dishes, baths, and bedtime would come and go, and I would fall into my bed again to sleep for a few hours. Then I'd be up, awake or not, with the twins for their midnight feeding.

I loved these little girls with all my soul, but the exhaustion overwhelmed me and tears filled my eyes. How long could I keep this up? Was I giving each of my children what they needed? Would there be anything left for me, of me? My mind wandered over the last ten years to the birth of our oldest child. I remembered the love that filled my heart when I held him in my arms the first time. I treasured him all the more now, and I cherished each of his siblings with the same intensity.

I looked down at Randi and Renae, still asleep on the floor. Randi shifted in her sleep and reached her little hand out toward her sister. Renae responded in kind, and soon they were holding hands as they slumbered. I couldn't imagine having one without the other. Their bond formed before birth, and I felt honored to be part of their lives. They would sleep through the night soon enough, and so would I. They would go to preschool before I knew it, and then they would be in school all day with the others. These precious moments of infancy wouldn't last, and I promised myself to enjoy each of them.

The twins started college this fall. How I miss them. I miss listening to their stories in stereo, the noise of teenagers in the house, the little girls they used to be. I miss the babies asleep on the living room floor, cuddling my sweet-smelling infants after their baths, staring into their eyes and seeing eternity mirrored there. With bittersweet emotion, I watch over them and my other four children from afar . . . and wait for grandchildren to hold in my arms.

Terry Deighton

The Cookie

At seven weeks, Ben was thriving; nursing constantly through a growth spurt, alert and interested in the world, smiling at his dad and me. He had just gotten control of his hands, and we laughed as we watched him wrap one hand around the other and, brow furrowed in concentration, push it into his mouth. "Self-soothing!" we crowed, and encouraged the behavior as best we could. It was hard to imagine a day when he would actually pick something up to put in his mouth.

Though Ben was doing well, I was a wreck. I spent my nights with him attached to me in bed, in the fitful, distracted sleep of someone with a new partner. "He's as engrossing and addictive as a new boyfriend," I confessed to a childless friend. "Except I made him." I spent my days with him in a sling, unable to put him down without his crying, subsisting on cheese toast and bananas and other snacks I could fix and eat with one hand while with the other I stroked his head or let him suck on my finger to give my aching breasts a break. I tried to remember any advice from my prenatal breastfeeding class—yes, the breastfeeding class. Tony and I had scoffed at the suggestion that breastfeeding could be taught, that there was, frankly, anything to teach. What, you just hold the baby up and it drinks, right? We'd waltzed into class a pair of know-it-all teenagers, only to come out two hours later, shell-shocked and awed at the incredible two-part system—baby and breast—that nourishes a child. I clung to the lactation consultant's metaphor like a life preserver: If you throw a person into a swimming pool, they'll probably get to the edge, but so much more easily if they know how to swim. We'd had our swim class; now Ben and I were trying not to drown.

I wailed on the phone to my older sister, who had successfully nursed two children. "Why doesn't anyone ever tell you? Nursing is harder than writing my dissertation!" She could sympathize, but from 3,000 miles away, she could offer no real help. Nor could my mother, who had nursed all four of us, but by the time she got to me (her youngest) also offered a honey-dipped pacifier. Meanwhile, my mother-in-law, surprised by two quick boys twenty years into her marriage, seemed simply to have blocked her memories of those chaotic days (though she did guiltily admit to a dry martini and a shrimp curry the night she went into labor with my husband). "No one ever suggested I breastfeed," she remarked, a bit wistfully. "It never occurred to me."

Talking to a friend one day (her son was just ten days older than Ben, so we commiserated daily), I learned of her mom's recent confession: When she'd been unable to stand it—the crying, the nursing, the sheer relentlessness of it all—any longer, she would just climb into the shower, leaving the baby lying on the bathroom floor. Often the steam and warmth would soothe the crying child, but if not, the noise of the shower would drown out the baby's cries. My friend and I were properly appalled at this old-fashioned approach.

But one day, at my wits' end and uncertain when I had last showered, I had to give it a try. I made Ben a cozy nest of towels on the bathroom floor. I stripped off my robe and underwear, unsnapped the nursing bra and let the milk-soaked nursing pads tumble out (I barely made it into clothing those days, but because of my steadily leaking milk supply, hardly ever took off the nursing bra). I climbed tentatively into the shower and pulled the door shut.

Ben, predictably, set up a wail. I turned the water up higher and began to sing. After a few moments, I realized he had fallen silent. *Had he suffocated?* I wondered. *Had he crawled (he couldn't even roll over) out of his nest and choked on a mouthful of terry?* I was so tired, it took me a moment to stop running disaster scenarios through my head, open the shower door, and with my heart in my mouth, check.

And there he was, legs kicking up in the air, one hand flailing, the other hand clutching a milk-soaked cotton nursing pad and stuffing it in and out of his mouth, cooing delightedly at his sweet prize, the inadvertent sugar cookie treat.

I watched my boy in wonder, the warm water splashing over my shoulders, and felt a sense of relief and pride wash over me. *We'll make it,* I thought.

That afternoon as Ben snoozed in his crib, I baked a batch of cookies to celebrate.

Caroline Grant

Of Their Own Design

Benjamin peered from his blue receiving blanket, his two-day-old face bewitchingly beautiful with bright eyes, tiny nose, and rosebud mouth.

"He looks like a monkey," Tami, my blond, wispy-haired four-year-old, announced as she took her first look at her new brother.

I'd conjured a thousand images of the moment Tami, my firstborn, would meet our new baby. None of my images included the disappointment now clouding Tami's blue eyes.

"Newborns do look a bit like monkeys," I said, determined to keep a positive tone although Ben didn't fit her description at all.

Ben opened his tiny mouth and let out a newborn cry. "He's probably hungry," I said. "If you bring a book, I'll read to you while I nurse him."

I settled into a corner of the couch, while Tami trotted into her bedroom for a book. I sighed with contentment as I gathered my new baby to nurse and patted a place beside me for Tami to sit while I read to her. This was more like what I wanted.

Nearly three weeks passed peacefully. When Ben cried, I picked him up to nurse. At those times, Tami promptly left her play with her Disney Enchanted Tales or Legos to fetch a favorite book and then climbed up beside me. Sometimes she touched Ben's cheek with one finger. "Hi," she said once. And another time, "Do you like your lunch? Is it good?" Mostly, she just turned the pages of her book, snuggling against me as I read the story or talking about the illustrations. Ben paid no attention to her, but she didn't seem to mind.

Feeding Ben every three hours plus caring for an active four-year-old exhausted me, but a sense of well-being enveloped me too. Tami seemed to be adjusting to the loss of her only-child status.

Then one day when Tami climbed up beside me with a book, Ben quit nursing and whimpered. "Read this, Momma," Tami said, loud enough to drown out her brother as she opened the book.

Ben's whimpers turned to howls and his face flushed red.

"I'm sorry, sweetie. I'd better read to you another time," I told Tami as I carried Ben into the master bedroom. As soon as I closed the door and settled into the rocking chair, Ben quieted and nursed contentedly.

The bedroom door creaked open. Tami tiptoed in, walked over to us, and pushed her book under my nose. Ben quit nursing and began to cry again.

"I'll read to you as soon as I'm done here," I whispered to her. "Why don't you build a surprise for me with your Legos?"

My heart ached when I saw her misty eyes and slumped shoulders as she left the room, but I felt confident that in just a few hours we'd be back to our nursing-and-reading routine. Ben wasn't even a month old. He couldn't possibly be demanding time alone with me.

Yet in the days that followed, Ben consistently refused to nurse unless it was just the two of us in the bedroom. Tami held up bravely for nearly another month as over and over I left her alone while I cared for Ben. She had preschool two mornings a week and went to a friend's several times. When Ben napped, I often got out Play-Doh or fingerpaints, or Tami and I made cookies together. I made certain she had plenty of activities she enjoyed. But she cried more easily and was more demanding than usual and I knew she was hurt and frustrated.

As another month passed, Tami tried hard to be a good older sister. When Ben lay on the floor on his patchwork quilt, she dragged a red bandana across his terrycloth-clad chest and his cheeks to entertain him. She showed him "Simon" and her Fisher-Price house of little people. She shook a rattle above his head, played her xylophone for him, and lined up all her stuffed animals along his quilt, giving them pretend voices and making them dance. Yet, as Ben approached two months, he seldom gave her the smiles with which he now sometimes responded to his father and me. He would look intently at her as though studying her, but that wasn't satisfying to a four-year-old.

"When will he get fun?" she asked one day as she made kissing sounds to him, trying unsuccessfully to elicit a smile or coo.

"Soon," I promised, kneeling beside her and putting an arm around her waist, hoping I was right.

One afternoon, as I sat at the dining room table paying bills while Ben slept upstairs in his cradle and Tami was presumably playing peacefully in her room, I heard a loud thud followed by Ben's screams. I raced upstairs. Ben lay on the floor with Tami at his side frantically patting his back.

"His cradle tipped over by itself," she said, her face pale with fright. "I hardly touched it. Is he all right?"

I swooped up Ben and held him close as he wailed. "Cradles don't tip over by themselves," I told Tami, struggling to keep my voice even.

Perhaps she'd done nothing more than rock him too energetically, but what if she had deliberately tried to hurt him in retaliation for all the times he appeared to ignore her? I knew brothers and sisters who bickered constantly growing up and as adult siblings flatly avoided each other. Were my children already heading in that direction? What could I do to help them enjoy each other? Who could advise me? Was there a book I hadn't already read that might have some ideas?

Over the next months, my husband and I gave Tami more attention, and she seemed happy enough with her friends and us, but she kept her distance from Ben. He was more active now, waving his arms and legs, gurgling, and starting to reach for things. Nearing five months, he was developing a real personality. Tami might have won a response from him at that point if she'd lain beside him and played with him as she had done before. But she seemed unwilling to risk rejection or blame for a mishap.

Then, one evening as I was making a salad, I heard Ben squeal. I spun around in time to see Tami dragging him by one sleeper-encased leg along the hardwood floor toward the kitchen. With a cry of horror, I took a step toward Tami, intending to swoop up Ben and send his torturer to her room for the longest time-out of her life. Then I noticed Ben's face. His eyes sparkled. He smiled the biggest smile I'd seen on his little face. The squeals were shrieks of joy.

"Look, Momma," Tami crowed. "He likes it. I'm being careful not to hit anything."

He did like it. I drew in a deep breath. I wanted to snatch my baby from any possible danger, and I'm sure no other mother and no book on parenting would have recommended their particular game for sibling bonding. I'd have to make sure they discovered other, safer activities to share. But I saw, as I slowly exhaled, that Tami was being careful not to bang Ben into anything and not to let his head bump along. Ben's diaper-clad bottom was well padded, and he slid easily from room to room. I understood for the first time that Tami and Ben would find their own ways, not necessarily of my design, to build a special sister-brother relationship.

Samantha Ducloux Waltz

The Mom Memory Lapse

When I brought my firstborn, Joey, home from the hospital, I had no idea what I was doing. I'd only been around babies once or twice in my life, so my mom, a seasoned mother of four, happily agreed to lend a hand for the first few days. Imagine my surprise (though, technically, it was more like panic) when my mother said, "I don't really remember that," every time I asked a question—particularly those pertaining to bottle-feeding.

It was bad enough that I'd opted to bottle feed. I had Joey at the beginning of the breastfeeding-is-beautiful movement. And those of us who chose the bottle were taken to task by just about everyone. The pediatricians told us we were risking our baby's antibody health. Nursing mothers warned that we wouldn't have that super-special bond with our baby.

But I stood my ground. So, when it was time to leave the hospital, I grabbed my free cans of formula, prefilled bottles, and a sticky note with instructions and clinked my way out of there as fast I could shuffle. I knew that my dear mother would be at home, ready to answer all those questions I hadn't the nerve to ask at the hospital. After all, Mom had bottle-fed her brood. Good old mom would come through for me.

"Mom," I asked, "how much of this formula should I give Joey?"

Mom looked at the mini-bottle and frowned. "I don't really remember that," she said.

"Mom, is it okay to give him the bottle again if he drinks only a little this time?" I asked, wondering about germs and such.

"Um, I don't really remember that," she said again.

"Mother," I asked, my anxiety building, "how often do you think I should feed Joey?"

Mother crinkled her brow. "Oh dear, that was a long time ago. I don't really remember that."

Sheeeesh. I hadn't been home for three hours, and already, I was worried that my baby wouldn't survive the night. There was nothing else to do but call the doctor's office. A very nice nurse patiently explained the answers to all my questions. "I feel like such an idiot," I said, apologetically.

"Oh, that's okay, every new mother feels like that," the nurse said.

I guess I felt better. I know Joey felt better after he got the right amount of formula at the right intervals. In fact, we all felt so much better about the baby situation that my husband and I decided to have another child soon after. And we didn't stop there. We added a third to the mix a few years later.

By that time, I was an old pro, right? It wasn't as if I were a brand-new mother who'd just fallen off the birthing bed. So when I brought newborn John home, my mother left before I even vacated my hospital room. My husband dropped me off at our house, then left in a rush to get back to work. The other two children were at schools of some sort. So there we were, just me and the baby.

No problem. I pulled one of the little prefilled bottles out of my bag and fed my new son.

When the children returned home from school an hour or so later, John woke up, ready to be the center of attention.

"Can we feed the baby?" asked Joey and his sister, Laney.

"Sure," I said.

Now, don't worry. I was there the whole time, overseeing the production, watching John as he sucked another bottle dry.

My husband finished work early and was home in time for the next feeding. I felt so good, I went to the kitchen to fix dinner.

"Should I give him the whole bottle?" my husband called from the family room.

"Fine," I said, stirring a pot.

The other two kids sat at the kitchen table with homework. It was a Norman Rockwell scene of family bliss . . . until a stream of formula shot from the family room all the way to the kitchen doorway.

My husband sat on the couch, bottle in hand, yelling for help. Poor little John looked okay, all things considered. But I was definitely not okay. I was ticking off a mental list of diseases that cause projectile vomiting. Picture me knee-deep in baby puke and hysteria.

"Maybe it was just too much formula?" my husband ventured.

I glared at him across the room while speed-dialing the pediatrician's office. The doctor came on the line immediately.

"How much formula is John taking in?" he asked.

I grabbed the bottle. "Four ounces," I said.

"Total?"

"No, no, at each feeding," I stammered. Why were we wasting time on formula questions when this kid probably had a blocked large intestine? Or was it an esophagus emergency?

"How many feedings has he had?" continued the doctor.

"Two. No, three. Wait . . . four? Yes, that's it, four. Every two hours," I was practically shouting.

There was a slight pause. "Mrs. Hall," said the doctor, "you are overfeeding that baby." He calmly explained the correct number of formula ounces John should be drinking and the proper feeding intervals.

"John's okay," I told my husband after hanging up the phone. I snatched the bottle and started cleaning the floor. "It was just too much formula," I mumbled, shooting him a don't-say-a-word look.

Oh, well. Old mom or new mom, I guess it doesn't much matter. I'll bet every mom has a few things to learn all over again every time she brings a new baby home. Come to think of it, I'm still learning new things about my children every day. And sometimes I'll call my mom with questions. Even though I know exactly what she'll say: "Honey, I don't really remember that."

Cathy C. Hall

Amazon Queen Takes a Hike

It's three o'clock in the morning, and I am pacing the floors, irritable and upset. I am not my usual self. I've become a moody, weepy bundle of nerves. Although I haven't slept in thirty-six hours, I cannot blame my altered state on sleep deprivation. It goes much deeper than that. My world has collapsed, overthrown by a tiny infant no more than two days old. I look at the little bundle in my arms and feel a wave of love laced with a new emotion I cannot identify. My mind struggles to put a name to it, but I am interrupted by another cry from my new boss. Apparently, I'm not pacing fast enough.

Just two nights before, I had been in the hospital, exhausted but happy at the birth of my firstborn son. Parker was born healthy and strong after fifteen hours of labor. Just fifteen hours! That was better than I had expected. After spending nine months hearing about everyone's childbirth experience in graphic detail, I was prepared for an epic battle. But I had survived the big event relatively unscathed and claimed my prize. Holding my son to my chest, I felt like a conquering queen. I smiled at the world and thought to myself, *At last, the worst is over.*

In my hospital room, surrounded by nurses, family, and friends, I had felt content and confident. I had no clue how difficult the next few days would be for both of us! Like so many of the expectant mothers in my Lamaze class, I had assumed that childbirth would be the most painful ordeal facing my baby and me. Although I had read that some mothers went through the "baby blues" after their child was born, I was sure that I would not. How could I possibly be depressed if I had my heart's desire? But I found out that we new moms are very complicated, fragile creatures and do not always know the things that can undo us. For me, it began the day I arrived home from the hospital.

My mother sat in the front seat chattering happily while my husband Jay drove us home. In the backseat, I cradled Parker's soft little head and stroked his cheek. He seemed so small in that huge infant seat. Once home, Jay and I struggled to get him out of it, his tiny head wobbling this way and that as we removed the straps.

"Careful with his little arms," my mother clucked in the background.

"He's so beautiful," I cooed as I wrapped him in the receiving blanket.

Jay took out the camera and snapped a picture of the two of us.

"Here, let me get a picture of the new family," my mother laughed.

She took the camera, and Jay stepped into the camera's viewfinder. We took another picture by the front door and still another by the welcome banner Jay had pinned to the foyer. We were like paparazzi run amok! But Parker slept through all the snapshots like a tired rock star.

Inside the nursery, I gingerly settled Parker in the crib, and Jay set the camera on the dresser with a sigh. "Honey, I hate to leave you, but I have to get back to work." He had dropped everything when I'd gone into labor. "I need to check up on things."

My mother's brow wrinkled at the news. "I was supposed to take your brother's dog to the vet, but if Jay's not going to be here, maybe I should stay," she offered.

"Relax, both of you. I'll be fine," I assured them. I'd read all the books and even attended a few baby classes; how hard could it be? Feeling efficient and in control, I assured them both that I would be okay.

Reluctantly, they finally left, and I was alone with my sleeping infant for the first time. I was looking forward to spending some special time with Parker. I glanced down at my sweet little boy, swaddled in baby blue blankets, and smiled.

Since Parker was still sleeping, I went into the kitchen to get something to eat. I had gone into labor before I could go grocery shopping, so there was not much food in the house. I managed to scare up a bagel, and just as I stuck it into the toaster, Parker awoke with a cry. Excited to hear his voice and to prove my mothering skills, I went off to his room.

I looked at the clock and figured it was time for his next feeding. So I picked up my sweetie, sat down, and put him to my breast as the nurse had shown me. But Parker would not latch on. He didn't seem to want the breast. *Maybe he just needs a fresh diaper,* I reasoned. But even with a dry diaper, he continued to cry. Going down the list of possibilities, I decided to give him the pacifier, but he spit it out. I tried one of the little bottles of formula they had given me in the hospital, but Parker did not want that either. I rocked him and sang to him, but he kept wailing. I tried to reason with him, and when that did not work, I begged him. But he was having none of it.

Four hours later, the bagel was still in the toaster and Parker was still crying. No matter how I tried to calm him down, he would not stop crying. With each ear-piercing wail, my confidence crumbled further. When Jay finally walked in the door, I took one look at him and burst into tears myself. Jay took turns comforting us until the baby and I both drifted off to sleep, but not for long. Two hours later, I started the whole crazy process again, this time pacing the floor with my screaming infant son in my arms in the pre-dawn hours of the morning.

They say that the definition of insanity is doing the same thing over and over and expecting a different result. Well, I guess I'm crazy, because that's exactly what I was doing—nursing, changing, rocking, pacifying, swaddling, pacing—with the same result as before: an unhappy, crying baby.

Alone in my son's room in the middle of the night, I review the events of the day and wonder what happened to the conquering queen from just the day before. Where did she go? Apparently, she and her little bundle have been replaced by two crybabies. I'm crying because I want my sanity back. And Parker, well, I don't know what he wants, which is precisely the problem. *Maybe what he really needs is a new mommy*, I think. *One who actually knows what to do, how to get him to eat and soothe him to sleep.*

I walk my son from one end of the house to the other, feeling as shell-shocked as someone walking through a hurricane. It certainly feels like my life is in ruins. In reality (which wouldn't occur to me until later), Parker isn't crying only from hunger or discomfort any more than I am crying only because I am exhausted from lack of sleep. We are both responding to the same sudden and irrevocable change in our lives. This new life is overwhelming and scary for both of us. My son must adjust to his new environment, which is so cold and bright and unresponsive in comparison to his first home inside my womb. And I must adjust to a new set of responsibilities and insecurities.

Parker finally falls asleep and I trudge back to bed. Though I don't want to let the words form in my mind, because they seem so selfish, I can't help but think, *What have I done? I've made a mistake.* I feel like a horrible mother for even thinking this, but exhaustion and frustration have gotten the better of me. The truth is, I am resentful. This little person has invaded my life and turned it upside down. As I drift off to sleep, I ask myself, *If he's exactly what I wanted, why do I feel so bad?*

Each morning I wake up hoping to feel differently, but it's been a week and nothing has changed. Inside, I'm torn apart. I look at my son and think,

Yes, he is what I've always wanted. Then another wave of anxiety hits, and I cry out, "But it's so overwhelming!" I secretly think he has single-handedly ruined my life, yet I can't bear the thought of him not being there. On one hand, I envy those who are childless and carefree, and on the other, I wake every hour to check Parker's breathing, holding my own breath until I can see evidence of his.

Am I the only one with such a torrent of mixed emotions? I wonder. I watch Jay, and he seems happy with Parker. My mother also seems comfortable with Parker, thrilled to be a grandmother at last. She cradles his head as she bathes him for the first time, and I realize that I cannot enjoy doing these simple things because I'm worrying the whole time that I will drop him. I fear that the sense of dread I feel at the thought of caring for him twenty-four hours a day, every day, will never cease. I watch my mother's easy movements, and my own uneasiness increases.

"I'm worried Parker is not drinking enough milk," I tell her.

My mother looks him over as she dries him, "He seems all right to me, but why don't you try the breast pump?"

I put the pump to my nipple and turn it on. Pain shoots up my breast, and I yank off the pump. "I don't want this!" I scream. "I made a mistake! I don't want to be a mother!"

"How can you feel that way?" she asks, alarmed. "Isn't he what you wanted?"

I can only cry in response. Not knowing what to say or how to comfort me, she urges me to call my best friend.

I call Sheila and try to make small talk, but I can barely speak.

"Please come," I finally whisper into the receiver.

"I'll be right over," she says.

Sheila knows what's wrong, because she has three young children of her own. She arrives with smiles and a hug. Before Parker was born, my friend had tried to prepare me for motherhood by telling me some of her war stories, but at the time they had only seemed amusing.

Sitting in the rocking chair, sipping tea, I pour out all my fears and uncertainties to her. She listens and then tells me it was the same for her: "With my first child, I remember thinking that I must have done everything right the day before because she was still alive in the morning."

As she confides her own mistakes and fears and successes, the knot in my chest slowly begins to unravel. I realize that I don't regret having a baby;

I just regret becoming vulnerable. I am not the invincible Amazon queen, able to balance million-dollar budgets while breastfeeding and cooking dinner. I am afraid that, where it matters most, I could be proven inadequate. After all, what good is it to meet impossible deadlines and increase revenue a hundredfold, if I can't take care of my little boy?

Parker begins to cry, and my mother brings him to me. I do not breastfeed, though; instead, Sheila offers to bottle-feed him. But her movements are not smooth and effortless, like they are when she is combing her daughter's tangled hair. "I must be rusty!" she laughs.

Parker finally latches on to the silicone nipple and then quickly stops, crying in disappointment and frustration. His little mouth searches the air above him for my breast. My heart melts, and I take my son in my arms and feed him. No matter how little I know or how insecure I feel, he wants me. My son wants me. Suddenly, I feel much better.

Sandi Abbott

The Rope

When I looked over at the couch today, I saw myself—or at least I saw the ghost of myself, counting down the final days before my twins' birth day. I cried for me and the things I couldn't comprehend then. I didn't know basic things, such as how to hold a baby, or the depth of anger I could feel toward two toddlers. Yet, what I really didn't understand was how those two little primitive souls would wrest mine away so that it would forever sit in the palms of their hands, how every action or thought of mine would somehow lead back to them.

Things I used to do or not do somehow were bigger with them in the world. When I read a news account about a dead child, I would thank God it wasn't mine and instantly feel guilty that other parents had suffered such a loss. If I chose to ignore some public issue, I also refused to change society for my own offspring. Even running was more significant than before, not only to benefit me but also as a way to clear my head so I could mother them again or to model the importance of fitness.

My husband and I had spent a year on the quest to become parents. The first brief pregnancy led to feeling inconvenienced about sharing my body. Within a week after the positive pregnancy test, I'd lost that baby. I began to fathom how children change a person's viewpoint; this journey wasn't just about me and my body. I started to think of myself as a vessel and altered my ways for our future sons or daughters. I stopped drinking soda pop, began eating salads, and didn't skip vitamins anymore.

Several disappointing months and some medical interventions later, a nurse relayed good news: I was pregnant again. Within weeks, I also discovered I was carrying twins.

Because of my first loss, I tempered my joy with caution. One day I woke up bleeding. Though I knew I shouldn't miss an important work deadline, I had to choose to protect the babies by going to the doctor instead. The ultrasound and exam showed two healthy progressing fetuses, so I hung on and followed the doctor's advice, doing my part as well as I could.

This pregnancy I couldn't wait to "show" and slip into maternity clothes, reveling in proof that my body kept changing and nurturing the babies in my womb. While my body swelled, I thrived.

One night in my third trimester, I had a dream:

Large and pregnant, I pull myself across the Mississippi River, the great mother river of America, on a heavy rope. Looking down at the turbid brown waters moving under me, I realize I cannot turn back; I must either continue to the other side or drown. At last I reach land, exhausted and relieved. The shore recedes in the distance as I return to gaze across the watery barrier's flat expanse. The rope disappears. I must remain on this side of the channel.

I spent the final five weeks of my pregnancy clutching a proverbial rope.

At thirty-two weeks into the pregnancy, a test revealed that labor was imminent if something didn't change. The doctor prescribed medication and told me to pass my afternoons on the couch, feet over my heart. Twisting slightly, I would lie with my hands on my belly, counting contractions and monitoring movement. Duncan, my dog, would put his head on the huge pillow of my belly, and his large eyes would let me know when the babies moved. Sometimes, I would drift into fitful, dream-filled sleep. When awake, I would read—how to hold babies, how to nurse babies, how to handle two babies, how to give birth to babies, and how to be a mother. I got sick of reading about babies and realized that only holding my two babies would teach me what to do.

On that couch, I both dreaded and anticipated the coming birth. I no longer wanted to live in limbo. I had already given the twins my body; now, I wanted to see what they looked like and to smell their sweet breath. I was afraid, having held babies only a couple times. How could I hold two? I tried to convince myself that doing everything twice would make me an expert within days.

In the cool darkness of the basement, my old life slipped away, day by day. While I spent afternoons alone with my internal monologue, my husband worked at his office and attempted to keep his thoughts on his job.

At last, I reached the end of my rope. In the middle of labor, I considered quitting. All thoughts of interconnectedness fell away, replaced with other stronger ones: *This is my body, and I want to leave the hospital.* My husband kept counting. I repeatedly whined that my back hurt.

Then someone said, "It's time."

Other bodies (whose?) unceremoniously dumped mine onto a gurney mid-contraction. They pushed me down the hallway, hitting every pothole, I was convinced. Faces floated around the delivery room. The doctor pulled out Twin A, our daughter. Momentarily happy, I continued to feel great pain.

A petite doctor joined my doctor as they tried to turn Twin B from his breech position. I squealed like a pig as our son's will won over the doctors' wills. I did not worry for the boy; I felt as if I were ripping asunder. An anesthesiologist whispered for me to push (my husband says she shouted). My Lamaze class had not covered what to do in the case of a breech birth. Upon hearing the instruction, I pushed—hard. No longer stuck, my son walked into the world. I was trembling, but glad for respite.

For a moment, I continued to think only of myself—then, no more. Soon, I wanted to follow my husband out the door with the babies—to begin our new lives as parents and with our new babies.

My husband and I have since learned that there is more than one rope to hang on to and more than one river to navigate. The excursion that began with my body continues to take us both to places we had never planned to go. We can only hang on for dear life and try to enjoy the journey.

Trina Lambert

This Big Love

"Do you really think I'll be able to love this baby?" A thick panic stuck in my chest like tar as I asked my mom this question over the phone.

My due date was three days away, and I seriously doubted my ability to be a good mother. I truly did not believe I would have the capacity to love another human being as much as I suspected was going to be required.

"Robbie, relax. You won't be able to resist this baby. Go to sleep. I love you."

She hung up, and I felt empty. I lumbered out of bed to put away the headset and returned to bed. I rolled to my right side and stared at my husband with tears in my eyes.

"We are going to have a baby, and I don't know if I can love it."

Roger stroked my hair and kissed my cheek. His tenderness made me feel even worse, like no one was taking me seriously. What if I had this fatal flaw and couldn't love my own child? It was possible. I had read about it happening.

"Honey, do you love Rainie?"

"Yes, I love Rainie," I said. "But she's a dog."

"Exactly," he responded, quietly but firmly. "You love, utterly and completely, a dog that is annoying, barks at the wind, and is obsessed with sticks. You will be able to love this baby."

A glimmer of hope shone through the fear in my heart. I really did love Rainie. I'd even tried to carry her across a river to ensure her safety one time, and she was a water dog who swam better than I. Even so, I needed more reassurance.

"Really, you really think I'll be okay?"

Roger just laughed and kissed me on the lips. "We have only a few more nights left before this baby comes out and we won't be getting any sleep. Can we please sleep now? Besides, it is a little late in the game to be having this conversation."

I relented and kissed him back. He was right. There was nothing I could do tonight. This baby was coming out regardless, and I would just have to do the best I could. And I really did love my dog; maybe I would love this baby, too.

Three days later, after seventeen hours of labor, I didn't care if I loved the baby or not. I wanted it out and I wanted it out now. My labor had been pretty standard but with intense back pain. In reality, it felt like someone was trying to jam a two-by-four through my spine and crack me in half, but apparently that was normal.

I was terrified of needles, especially needles in areas of my body that were critical, like my spinal cord, so I had labored without the help of drugs. My water broke after sixteen hours, and instead of moving things forward, my cervix retracted a centimeter. I was sick of the doctors checking me and stating "still more cervix" and of my birthing team cheering me on like all I had to do was one more lap around the track. Again, people were not grasping the entirety of the situation. Apparently, they were dense and did not understand that I was done. As I lay on the bed for yet another discouraging check and heard the pep squad attempting to buoy my spirits on either side of me, I could take no more.

"Shut up," I said as I put my hand in my husband's face. "Stop talking. All of you!"

The crew silenced and stared at me. I turned my head to Dr. Wilber, my only hope for salvation from this unrelenting pain. "Doctor, give me drugs."

Dr. Wilber smiled calmly, and I knew all would be fine.

"We'll get you something as soon as we get you hydrated, Robin."

Ah, someone whom I could trust. Dr. Wilber understood.

The nurse appeared, and after the next contraction, she inserted an intravenous line into my right arm. Normally, I would have been terrified, but now I just chanted silently, *Drugs are coming, drugs are coming, drugs are coming.*

The fluids and mantra must have helped, because I relaxed. Then, I suddenly had this enormous pressure surge through my body, and I wanted to push like my life depended on it. I pushed and moaned with the force of it and felt almost liberated by being able to counter the agonizing contractions that had torn through me for so long. With each urge, I pushed with as much force as I could muster, and soon I heard cheers all around me.

"Just one more, Robin, one more. I can see her head," Dr. Wilber urged me on.

Summoning all my strength, I pushed until I felt the head emerging. *Finally,* I thought. *Finally, get out!* At that point, I felt nothing but adrenaline.

"Do you want to feel the head?" Dr. Wilber asked. "No! I just want it out!"

What was she thinking? This was not the time for touchy-feely experimentation. I wanted to be done. I almost lost it at that moment, another contraction snapped me back into action, and this time I felt the head slip out. Relief swept over me, all I could do was cry as they laid my newborn's tiny wet body on my chest.

"Congratulations! You have a . . . "

We had wanted Roger to announce the baby's gender, but in the excitement he had forgotten to check. He looked down and with tears said, "It's a girl. We have a little girl."

An emotion so big that it surpassed all the pain of the contractions coursed through me. Love. A love unlike any I'd ever felt before welled up so hugely in me that my heart cracked wide open. Overcome with love, I sobbed to be holding this baby, this child, this daughter of mine. I looked into her eyes, and she locked onto mine. I felt as if I had known this tiny creature my entire life.

"Hello, little girl," I whispered, tears streaming down my face. "I am so excited to meet you." I could hardly breathe as I kissed her head and held her close. "I am your momma, little girl. And I love you so much."

I finally understood what everyone had been trying to tell me. I could not resist this love for my daughter. This love was bigger than me. It was a gift from God. And it made everything else worthwhile.

Robin M. J. Dowdy

Tell Your Story in the Next
Cup of Comfort

We hope you have enjoyed *A Cup of Comfort® for New Mothers,* and that you will share it with the people in your life who bring you comfort. We're brewing up lots of other *Cup of Comfort®* books, each filled to the brim with true stories that will touch your heart and soothe your soul.

Do you have a powerful story about an experience that dramatically changed your life? A compelling story that can stir our emotions, make us think, bring us hope? Tell your story!

Each *Cup of Comfort®* contributor will receive payment, author credit, and a free copy of the book. Just e-mail your submission of 1,000 to 2,000 words (one story per e-mail; no attachments, please) to *cupofcomfort@adamsmedia.com* or send it to:

A Cup of Comfort
Adams Media Corporation
57 Littlefield Street
Avon, Massachusetts 02322

Make sure to include your name, address, and other contact information. We also welcome your suggestions or stories for new *Cup of Comfort®* themes. For more information, please visit *www.cupofcomfort.com.*   *319*

Contributors

Sandi Abbott ("Amazon Queen Takes a Hike") resigned her position as a marketing wonder woman to take on the challenging roles of writer and home-schooling mom. Now she battles with long division by day and writes for print and television by night. She lives in Miami, Florida, with her husband and two children.

Kristina J. Adams ("Mirroring Mom") is a sixth-grade social studies teacher who grew up in Austria, Turkey, and Germany before finishing high school in Illinois. She resides in Goshen, Indiana, with husband, Ryan, and children Mackenzie and Carter. In 2003, she had her first story published in an anthology and has had several articles published in *Among Worlds* magazine.

Tammera Ayers ("Delivering Hope") works part-time as a community services coordinator for senior independence and also participates in the community farmers' market, making noodles and apple dumplings. She lives in St. Marys, Ohio, with her husband, three teenagers, and an array of animals. In her spare time, Tammera enjoys writing, reading, and gardening.

Janine Boldrin ("And I Pray for Baby Ike") is a writer who lives at West Point, New York, with her family. Her stories have appeared in *A Cup of Comfort®* *for Breast Cancer Survivors* and *A Cup of Comfort®* *for Military Families*. Always in pursuit of a good night's rest, Janine hopes one day to be able to complete a thought and stop asking if anyone "needs to use the potty" every five minutes.

Laura L. Bradford ("Nesting") is a semi-retired caregiver who resides in Walla Walla, Washington. She enjoys encouraging others with her stories about faith and family. Her writings have appeared in *Life Savors, A Cup of Comfort®* *for Families Touched by Alzheimer's,* and the *Oregon Christian Writers Newsletter.*

Amanda Callendrier ("Pig Doo and Foofy") lives in a small village in the French Alps, despite being the world's worst skier and quite disinclined to learn. She works as a corporate English instructor and tries to find time to write amidst all the noise from her children.

Linda S. Clare ("All New Mommies See Double") is an award-winning writer, college writing instructor, and freelance editor in Eugene, Oregon, where she lives with her husband, their four adult children, and several wayward cats. She is the coauthor of three books, including *Lost Boys and the Moms Who Love Them, Revealed: Spiritual Reality in a Makeover World,* and *Making Peace with a Dangerous God.* Currently, she is working on a memoir about her experiences in a 1960s Shriners Children's Hospital, and a nonfiction book called *GodSong.*

Patricia L. Crawford ("Knit One, Hurl Two"), an Army veteran raised as an Air Force brat, has always loved to write. In fact, writing is her favorite part of the high school English class she teaches. Nothing in her life has given her as much material for her writing than her two wonderful sons, without whom this story and many others would not have been written.

LeeAnn Elder Dakers ("Bonded for Life"), a freelance journalist, lives in Oregon with her husband, Alec, and two remaining homebound sons, Kai and Keenan. Alex graduated from high school and moved out on his own in the fall. He promises to call his mom, "but not every day." LeeAnn has worked as a staff writer and editor at regional and international publications.

Shawn Daywalt-Lutz ("The Best-Laid Plans") lives in Capistrano Beach, California, with her husband, two children, and a variety of domestic animals. A retired actress and singer, Shawn enjoys being with her family, exploring California, and writing. This is her third publication in the *Cup of Comfort®* book series.

Terry Deighton ("Double Trouble") resides in Sedro-Woolley, Washington, with her husband, Al, and any number of their six children when they are on school break. She graduated from Brigham Young University in humanities teaching and is a substitute teacher. Terry is a member of American Night Writers Association.

Barbara D. Diggs ("A Tale of Two Mothers") is a freelance writer living in Paris, France, with her husband and son. A former corporate lawyer, Barbara practiced law in New York and Paris for several years before changing careers. In addition to writing for various magazines, she is currently writing a book about intercultural weddings.

Robin M. J. Dowdy ("This Big Love") is a parent, writer, life coach, educator, and business owner. She lives in Seattle, Washington, with her husband, two kids, and dog. Writing, yoga, coaching, and being outside are Robin's outlets. As a writer, she is deeply inspired by the work of Madeleine L'Engle.

Terri Elders ("Finding My Comfort Zone") lives near Colville, Washington. Her stories have appeared in several anthologies, including *Life Lessons for Living the Law of Attraction.* A licensed clinical social worker, she serves as a public member of the Washington State Medical Quality Assurance Commission. In 2006, she received the UCLA Alumni Award for Community Service.

Ann Friesen ("More Than Words") recently moved to Pennsylvania, where she lives with her husband and the youngest two of her six children. Previously a teacher in the private sector, she now divides her time among writing, outdoor activities, and mentoring college students.

Jodi Gastaldo ("Froggy Feet") resides in Cleveland, Ohio, with her husband, Dan, and two children, Maggie and Ben. When not reading or writing for pleasure, she works toward her dream of earning a nursing degree.

Erika Swanson Geiss ("Labor of Love") is an accomplished writer and editor. Her publication credits include books and articles in printed and electronic media. Geiss is the author of *The Right Words for Any Occasion* and the editor-in-chief of the *WAHMmagazine,* an e-zine. She and her husband, Doug, are raising Michael in the suburbs of Detroit, Michigan.

Elizabeth King Gerlach ("The Sisterhood of Motherhood") is the proud mama and step-mama of four boys. She has written two award-winning books on autism and has two children's books awaiting publication. This is the fifth of her stories to be published in the *Cup of Comfort*® book series. She lives in Eugene, Oregon.

Caroline Grant ("The Cookie") is Senior Editor of *Literary Mama,* where she also writes the monthly column, "Mama at the Movies." She is coeditor of *Mama, PhD: Women Write about Motherhood and Academic Life.* She lives in San Francisco with her husband and two sons, all of whom love cookies.

Abigail Green ("Taking Care") is a freelance writer specializing in health, parenting, and essays. She has published more than 150 articles in magazines, newspapers, and online, and writes about the lighter side of motherhood in her blog, Diary of a New Mom. She lives with her husband and toddler son in Baltimore.

Jennifer Gunter ("Power Eating") is an OB/GYN and the mother of Oliver and Victor, who were born at twenty-six weeks' gestation. After several difficult years, they are now thriving and, as predicted, proving to be stiff competition around the dinner table. She lives with her three boys (husband included) in Northern California and is currently working on her first book, a survival guide for parents with premature babies.

Cathy C. Hall ("The Mom Memory Lapse") is a freelance writer from Lilburn, Georgia. Her humorous essays have appeared in magazines, newspapers, and anthologies. She is currently trying her writing hand with children's fiction. Her story "The Chocolate Cake Bait" was a recent winner in the Alabama Writer's Conclave competition.

Kristi Hemingway ("Maternity Revisited" and "Where's a New Mother to Turn?") is a writer, a teacher of speech and theater, and a performing artist. Her greatest role to date has been as mother to Levi and Eden. Her family currently lives in Denver, Colorado, but dreams of Southern France. She has written books, contributed to anthologies, and enjoys freelancing for children's, family, and travel magazines.

Amy Hudock ("Learning to Breathe"), a single mother and writer, is the co-founder of the e-zine *Literary Mama* and the co-editor of *Literary Mama* as well as the book *American Women Prose Writers, 1820–1870*. Her work has appeared in *Mama PhD*, *A Cup of Comfort® for Single Mothers*, *Single State of the Union*, and other anthologies.

Nancy Ilk ("Mother's First Year") is a writer and homemaker living in Oak Creek, Wisconsin, with her husband and yellow lab, Gracie. Her short stories and essays have appeared in anthologies as well as in several online publications. She is currently working on her first children's book.

Kelly James-Enger ("I'm Having a Baby . . . Really!") writes and speaks about getting and staying healthy and stress-free. Her books include *The Belated Baby: A Guide to Parenting after Infertility* (with Jill S. Browning). She's also Ryan's mommy and Erik's wife, and lives outside Chicago with her family.

Mimi Greenwood Knight ("Mom Overboard!" and "That's What Friends Are For") is a South Luziana girl and freelance writer who enjoys butterfly gardening, Bible study, the lost art of letter writing, and—on a good day—her husband. She has more than three hundred published articles and essays in magazines, anthologies, and websites. Mimi is now happily stumbling through her grocery trips with four kids in tow, always on the look-out for newer moms in need of validation.

Trina Lambert ("The Rope") writes essays, articles, and commentaries from her home in Colorado. She and her husband, Sherman, have been navigating their parenting journey for more than sixteen years. As their children prepare to leave the nest, Trina and Sherman look forward to discovering where the journey will go next.

Denise K. Loock ("Imperfect, Not Incompetent") is an adjunct English professor and a freelance writer. She lives in New Jersey with her husband, two teens, her eighty-five-year-old mother, and two cats. She loves summertime—gardening, Yankee games, and outdoor grilling.

Mary-Kate Mackey ("Ripple Effect") is a recipient of a Garden Writers Association Silver Award of Achievement for magazine writing. Her articles have appeared in *Fine Gardening*, *Sunset*, and she is a contributor to the 2007 *Sunset Western Garden Book*. She teaches at the University of Oregon's School of Journalism and Communication. With her husband, Lou Favreau, she has raised two children in Eugene, Oregon.

Leeann Minogue ("Feeding Jackson") lives with her husband and young son on a grain farm in southern Saskatchewan, Canada. Leeann's first play, *Dry Streak*, has made people laugh in several Saskatchewan theaters. She is currently writing during naptimes to finish a second play.

Amy Nathan ("Mothering from Scratch") lives and writes near Chicago. She is published in the Chicago *Tribune* and very cool parenting books, magazines, and journals nationwide. In addition to writing a novel, Amy spends her days in awe of Zachary and Chloe, who, as teenagers, both sleep late on weekends.

Anna Packham ("Light of My Life") is a writer and runs a copywriting firm from her home in Brighton, England. Her stories have been featured in *Long Story Short, Tales of the Decongested, Voracity Beat,* and *Scarlet* magazine. She finds being a mother (and life) to be eye-opening, thrilling, magic, petrifying, insane, and incredibly joyful.

Kelli Perkins ("Welcome Home") earned a master's degree in early childhood education from Virginia Commonwealth University and taught fourth grade before becoming a full-time mom. She and her husband have been married for twelve years and have two amazing kids. She is now pursuing her childhood dream of becoming a writer and is excited to make her writing debut in *A Cup of Comfort® for New Mothers*.

Susan Lynn Perry ("The Big Blowout") is an accomplished writer and frequent contributor to the *Cup of Comfort®* book series. In addition to writing numerous published articles, short stories, novels, and nonfiction books, she is the author of *Mother Cub*, an uplifting account of the challenges and joys involved in helping her young son emerge from autism.

Caroline B. Poser ("Hello, Baby—Goodbye, Body"), a Massachusetts mother of three sons, works full-time as a software marketing professional and moonlights as an author and columnist. Her first book, *MotherMorphosis®*, was endorsed by *Parenting Magazine* editor Julie Tilsner as well as Jane Swift, the first governor in U.S. history to give birth while in office.

Kristina Riggle ("Small Sacrifices") is a freelance writer in West Michigan. The writing she did in coffee shops and during frantic bursts while her baby napped turned into her debut novel, *Real Life and Liars* (due out in spring 2009). She is the fiction coeditor for the e-zine *Literary Mama* and has published short stories in *Cimarron Review* and other publications.

Kendal Seager ("Tooth by Tooth") stumbled happily into motherhood while residing in a haunted hotel in Portland, Oregon. While she considers Portland home, she currently lives with her family in Los Angeles, California, where she intends to learn the art of riding waves while standing on a plank of wood and live to write about it. She is eternally grateful to be her daughter's mother.

Julie Sharp ("For Crying Out Loud") is a stay-at-home-mom from San Clemente, California. She loves anything that tests her patience: word puzzles, scrapbooking, cross-stitching, and the San Diego Chargers. Julie is madly in love with her husband, Grant; son, PJ; and first love, Jesus Christ. They are the inspiration for her writing, hope for her future, and joy in her heart.

Deanna Stollar ("Under a Starlit Sky") resides with her husband, Terry, in Springfield, Oregon. They raised four children and cared for three foster children. A lecturer, freelance writer, and Christian home educator, Deanna is the author of *It Takes a Parent*, coauthor of *Coaching Policy Debate*, and contributor to *A Cup of Comfort® for Horse Lovers*.

Sharon A. Struth ("Beware of Shifting Tides") is a freelance writer who lives in Bethel, Connecticut, with her two teenage daughters, two dogs, and husband of twenty years. Her work can also be seen in *Sasee* magazine.

Kimberly Thompson ("Equal to the Task"), of Lindon, Utah, is the mother of six beautiful children. She earned a bachelor's degree in business management and owns an online scrapbooking company, Kim's Scrapshack. She loves to write, read, scrapbook, and cook. A personal and professional blogger, she also writes media reviews and recently submitted her first novel.

Cristy Trandahl ("Simply Perfect") works as a freelance writer while raising six beautiful children. Her stories are published in dozens of nationally distributed anthologies.

Stacy Voss ("Cordless") lives in Highlands Ranch, Colorado, with her husband, Allen, and children, Micayla and Gabe. She is a mom by day and a development consultant and freelance writer by night. Stacy loves running, hiking, camping, and spending time with her family.

Samantha Ducloux Waltz ("Of Their Own Design") is an award-winning freelance writer in Portland, Oregon. Her essays can be seen in the *Cup of Comfort®* series, the *Chicken Soup for the Soul* series, and a number of other anthologies, as well as *The Rambler* and other magazines. Tami and Ben live in Portland, as well, still nurturing a strong sister-brother bond.

Mary Jo Marcellus Wyse ("Battle of the Breast" and "The Night and the New Mom") is a graduate of Vermont College's MFA in writing program. Her recent writing credits include *Iddie, Lunarosity, Jerry Jazz Musician, Italy from a Backpack, Current Magazine,* and *Mota 4: Integrity*. A former English teacher at North Pole High School in North Pole, Alaska, she is now a happy stay-at-home mom to a sweet little boy.

About the Editor

Colleen Sell has compiled and edited twenty-eight volumes of the *Cup of Comfort*® book series. She has authored, ghostwritten, and edited numerous books; published scores of articles; and served as editor-in-chief of two award-winning consumer magazines. She and her husband, T. N. Trudeau, share an ancient farmhouse, which they are perpetually renovating, on forty acres, which they are slowly turning into a lavender farm, in the Pacific Northwest.